ENDORSEMENTS

T0025801

Back in the summer of 1991, while living in Argentina I remember one day walking into our office to find Steve prostrate on the floor crying out to God. This was very normal in our house, but this time what I heard him saying was *so* intense. He was saying, *"God, I don't want to work for You in my own strength...I want You to do Your work through me."* I backed out and sat down in the hall engulfed in God's presence and started crying and agreeing saying, *"Yes God, do it Lord, hear his cry, oh God."* Serving God before that day had been very exciting and fruitful, but God birthed in us that day a hunger for *more*. We wanted it to be so evident that the things done through our lives and ministry could only be done by God Himself. My prayer is that this book, *The Fire That Never Sleeps*, will stir in everyone who reads it a hunger for God—that they will fight through every distraction to obtain it.

JERI HILL
President of Steve Hill Ministries
Wife of the late Evangelist, Steve Hill

In *The Fire That Never Sleeps*, Dr. Michael Brown, John Kilpatrick, and Larry Sparks help us understand what revival really means. I deeply respect these men of God and am grateful for the part they played in the Brownsville Revival. Dr. Brown writes with such clarity and anointing, dedicated to seeking the truth. Each one of us should be pursuing revival in our lives and on the earth with passion to see God's love and power in greater measure.

HEIDI G. BAKER, PHD
Co-founder and Director of Iris Global

I believe that in her latter days the Church will witness the presence and power of God to a degree we have never known before. This display of God's glory will be ushered in as we consecrate ourselves and seek Him—His presence, His purpose, and His fame—above all else.

Does your heart long to see a greater manifestation of God's Kingdom on the earth? Then I pray that the stories and principles contained in this book will ignite in you a passion that alters your life forever.

JOHN BEVERE
Author and minister
Messenger International

A great spiritual awakening is coming to America. This book will make sure it doesn't pass you by!

SID ROTH
New York Times bestselling author
Host, *It's Supernatural!*

Three great minds, each touched by the fire of God, have put their hearts together to relive those awesome times when the Holy Spirit invaded earth. Specifically, the site was Pensacola, Florida, and what we remember as the Brownsville Revival.

Twenty years later, those of us who were there will vividly recall its glory as we read *The Fire That Never Sleeps*. Others who came later can experience it vicariously in this wonderful memorial book. Thank God for these writers and the Holy Spirit who motivated them to put these "stones of memory" in our lives!

CHARLES CARRIN
President, Charles Carrin Ministries
Author of *The Edge of Glory* and
co-author of *Word, Spirit, Power*

I am one of the multiple thousands who came running to the mercy seat and met Jesus at the altars in Brownsville. Decades later, the fire from that encounter still burns within me. This is the lasting testament of a genuine move of God. The fruit of the revival is clearly seen in the transformed lives of those who responded to messages; the missionaries who were sent out; the evangelists who, like Steve Hill, boldly preach the truth; and within the churches that continue to burn with God's holy presence.

Pastor Kilpatrick, Dr. Brown, and Larry Sparks have penned some of the burning embers from Brownsville into a book that the dry and thirsty can cast upon their soul. The same flames that touched millions at Brownsville are now waiting to touch you. *The Fire That Never Sleeps* is not just about what God did, it's about what He is doing and how you cultivate and sustain a move of God in your own life.

DANIEL K. NORRIS
Evangelist with Steve Hill Ministries

Dr. Michael Brown and Pastor John Kilpatrick's new book, *The Fire that Never Sleeps: Keys to Sustaining Personal Revival,* is an amazing book that one would expect from two figures who are so experienced in revival. I found the book enlightening and encouraging, both inspiring and instructive. It is a book I will carry on our book tables for our forthcoming Schools of Revival. It is well written and important for now. I believe God is getting the Church ready for another outpouring of the Spirit. This is a book you should have in your library.

RANDY CLARK, DMIN.
Founder and President of Global Awakening and
the Apostolic Network of Global Awakening

Pastor John Kilpatrick and Dr. Michael Brown are uniquely qualified to speak about revival, having been used by God to spearhead one of the greatest outpourings in modern times. Together with Larry Sparks, they have written a book that manages to convey not only the principles but also the spirit of revival that indelibly marked my own life many years ago. Although the public meetings have long since ended, the fire still burns within me. *The Fire That Never Sleeps* is more than a good read—it is a catalyst for your own personal ongoing, lifelong revival.

DANIEL KOLENDA
President and CEO, Christ for All Nations
Author of *Live Before You Die*

In *The Fire That Never Sleeps*, John Kilpatrick and Michael Brown relate their passion of how, through prayer, commitment to integrity, and faithfulness over years, revival came and remained. Godly, passionate lives surrendered to the presence of the Holy Spirit can lead to sustained and nation-changing revival. Listen to these men carefully; the Brownsville Revival changed the world. And Evangelist Steve Hill is shining from the battlements of Hheaven right now with a gigantic "Amen!"

JOHN ARNOTT
Founding Pastor and President, Catch the Fire
Author of *The Father's Blessing*

This book is a real gem. The authors have successfully revealed the crisis of compromised religion along with the call to return to normal Christianity marked by God's continual divine presence. I am a product of the Brownsville Revival and a sign of its lasting fruit. It is my pleasure to fully endorse this book as a guide to all those who long to experience the presence and glory of God.

PASTOR STEVE GRAY
Pastor, The Smithton Outpouring and World Revival Church

I visited the Brownsville Revival with great blessing and rejoiced in the continuing news of its progress. *Fire* is a proper identification of genuine revival. Admitting this, we acknowledge that revival is never static; it's always active and ever-changing. The fire never really goes out. The testimony of its value is in the lives around the world that were and are being altered.

The telling of the story by Michael Brown and John Kilpatrick is one of efficient explanation, honest evaluation, and inevitable celebration.

I never read the story of revival without entering into a chain reaction of memories spanning half a century of study of historic moves of God and experiencing the fire still burning.

Larry Sparks has skillfully guided this project, and John and Michael are to be commended for a work that will provide us and yet unborn generations with a story that never ends.

I have a tear in my heart as Steve Hill's face and voice still resound in my memory. His going seemed too soon to us...but living large is better than living long, and Steve truly lived large to see God's Kingdom populated. The presence of his influence touches this whole volume and is a fitting tribute to a life well lived.

JACK TAYLOR
Dimensions Ministries
Melbourne, Florida

THE

FIRE

KEYS FOR
SUSTAINING
PERSONAL
REVIVAL

THAT NEVER
SLEEPS

MICHAEL L. BROWN
& JOHN KILPATRICK
WITH LARRY SPARKS

DESTINY IMAGE® PUBLISHERS, INC.

P.O. Box 310, Shippensburg, PA 17257-0310

"Promoting Inspired Lives."

This book and all other Destiny Image and Destiny Image Fiction books are available at Christian bookstores and distributors worldwide.

Cover design by Eileen Rockwell

For more information on foreign distributors, call 717-532-3040.

Reach us on the Internet: www.destinyimage.com.

ISBN 13 TP: 978-0-7684-0718-1

ISBN 13 eBook: 978-0-7684-0719-8

For Worldwide Distribution, Printed in the U.S.A.

IN MEMORY OF
EVANGELIST STEVE HILL
(1954–2014),
THE MAN GOD USED TO IGNITE
THE BROWNSVILLE REVIVAL.

*The fire on the altar shall be kept
burning on it; it shall not go out.*
—LEVITICUS 6:12

*God's fire only falls on sacrifice. An
empty altar receives no fire!*
—FRANK BARTLEMAN

CONTENTS

FOREWORD

This book is a confronting message of Love *for*—and a humbling appeal *to*—*the Church*. The *whole* Church. Its timing is right, because we are *all* "near midnight."

Ironically, though written in love, this book is sorely at risk of being judged as negative and critical; as a splash of cold water in your face, rather than being handed to you like a Starbucks latte to ease you into another day.

I urge you—*read it anyway.*

It may agitate you before it comforts, or irritate before it personally concerns *you*. I join myself with that *you,* because we are *all* inclined to perceive this book's message as one "for someone else," or as "not my style."

Upon careful reflection, there are three reasons why you should engage this timely offering from Dr. Michael Brown, Pastor John Kilpatrick, and Larry Sparks, *The Fire That Never Sleeps*:

1. *Renewal*: It serves as a personal call to renewal in both passion and repentance. There is a great need for next-generation leaders to consider the ministry call they are being served. While methods may change, the message is timeless. Reader, you will truly be summoned to reconsider what a New Testament discipleship lifestyle looks like and how it impacts the course of everyday living.

Discipleship demands discipline, and such discipline is not an open door into a lifestyle of legalism or joylessness. Quite the contrary, *The Fire That Never Sleeps* paints a vivid picture of how revival is nothing short of New Testament discipleship. To be a disciple of Jesus, you are, by default, *reviving* what was considered normal during the first century. You will learn how to engage powerful practices such as:

- **Prayer** that enters into the Veil and intercedes with steadfastness.

- **Worship** that breaks with the shallowness of mere "entertainment" and draws believers into life-changing encounters with God; a readiness to receive the Word; and a heart to live, love, and serve as "agents of the Kingdom" in their homes, neighborhoods, or workplaces—not to mention their local congregations.

- **Surrender** to the Holy Spirit's fullness—poured out to be received as a "River," overflowing with power, purity, and the pungency of "Christ in you!"

2. *Remembrance*: This work brings to my remembrance the dynamic work that God performed on a global scale during the Brownsville Revival. It brought to mind my meeting and awareness of Pastor John Kilpatrick's experience (*and* his sensitive and sensible pastoral leadership alongside Steve Hill). Truly, he was a pastor of revival, as he maintained a solid, scripturally wise balance amid the drama, dynamic, and demands of such a victorious advance of the Kingdom.

John and Steve, along with Michael Brown, were a "trinity" of sorts that banded the distinct giftings of each and not only cut a swath of Kingdom ministry (people saved, healed, delivered, and then many, many entered), grew, and became established as disciples—people *following Jesus* in their walk, not simply "Getting their needs met and becoming excitable, though hardly teachable."

3. *Response.* This book is not merely a memorial of what "once was," but offers scriptural strategies on how to personally respond to the call of revival. The Brownsville Revival cannot be measured by how long services continued uninterrupted at Brownsville Assembly of God in Pensacola, Florida. I know some measure revival by this standard. Rather, we evaluate the full effect of revival by examining the lives of pastors, leaders, and believers who were touched by the fire and have been living on fire ever since.

This is where I must urge you, dear reader—respond correctly. There are a host of pastors across the nation who were either passé or critical toward Brownsville. They resisted the "witness" of God's great work and instead sought His presence, power, and purpose in their own congregations, believing it unnecessary to "go elsewhere to experience God." While I would agree that location is irrelevant to receiving a touch from God, humility is essential.

Many excused their passivity and criticism as their effort to "avoid extremism." In turn, they assumed an extreme posture of either suspicion or scorn concerning such a move of God—never bothering to *look* into the actualities of the revival or their own need as leaders to give a larger place to the Holy Spirit's move being welcomed in their own lives and their congregations.

Response is everything, as it directly impacts what we receive from God.

It was nearly fifty years ago—in reading a book that probed my soul in ways similar to this one—that I learned this "sensible thing": *It is absolutely essential to remain aware of my vulnerability to becoming a Pharisee.* They were a breed of religious leaders, doubt-lessly sincere, but also had become so fixated on their presumed "absolute correctness and purity," in understanding and style of dutifully "doing" service for God, that they never really understood God in Person. Consequently, when God showed up personally, in His Son Jesus Christ, His confrontation with their "style"—however dedicated—was rejection, and God Himself was thereby unable to influence, help, or shape these "righteous experts" beyond the "patterns of their perfection."

To my view, the spirit prompting *The Fire That Never Sleeps* is the same spirit, and with the same spiritual passion as earlier voices to the Church like Leonard Ravenhill, Vance Havner, David Wilk-erson, and, presently, Jim Cymbala. Such voices—though often boldly and forthrightly *calling out* those who know Christ yet linger behind Him unwittingly or with known indifference—are essential to us all.

Such messengers, as well as the message here, are not given to lash, but to lead us—to point freshly to our *Savior,* to a kneeling again to honor Him as *Lord,* and as the soon-to-return Bridegroom of the Church. The objective is benevolent—the directness of speech targeted only to seek the fruitfulness of those who love Him and our readiness to meet Him without shame at His appearing. Accordingly, I perceive nothing in this book intending self-righteous criticism or condescension. However, there *is* a forthright candor that cuts at our flesh with a trumpet-like alert that will disallow casual hearing and prohibit drowsiness or sleep.

However, the issues addressed here are needed by us all. Nothing has become more commonly blurred or lost, in the culture at large as well as in the Church, as a clear-eyed, discerning perspective on the difference between *style* and *substance*. This is no insult to anyone's intelligence; it's a liability that often takes a "shock treatment" to call us back to "Go!" To the "Go" in Jesus's Commission, which is richer and deeper in scope and substance than commonly seen today.

And as needful as the "comfort" of God's Spirit is—as "the Comforter" is preferred—He is just as adept at *convicting* as He is at consoling us...and we need *both*.

As for *this* book, at age 28—early in my pastoral/teaching ministry—it was one very much like this one that became pivotal to my life to this very day. It ignited a passion, but it also instructed toward a pathway. I learned that I needed to be slow to dismiss speakers or writers who were not to my taste or style. If their words or ways irritated me (or "burned me up") I need to "tune in before I turned them off."

I learned that the heat of a flame that burns your fingers can't be held, but it will get your full attention; and, however unpleasant the burn, the outcome may very well cause you to handle things more cautiously and wisely than you did before. Such "temporary burns" can awaken a *sensitivity* that can shape a lifetime of deeper *sensibility*.

This book's pages strongly brought the following four scriptural statements to mind, riveting my personal sense of renewed accountability and sensitivity to take heed with faithfulness, humility, and dependency on God to keep the fire burning:

You have been weighed in the balances, and found wanting (Daniel 5:27).

And to the angel of the church in Sardis write, "These things says He who has the seven Spirits of God and the seven stars: 'I know your works, that you have a name that you are alive, but you are dead. Be watchful, and strengthen the things which remain, that are ready to die, for I have not found your works perfect before God. Remember therefore how you have received and heard; hold fast and repent. Therefore if you will not watch, I will come upon you as a thief, and you will not know what hour I will come upon you." (Revelation 3:1-3 NKJV).

And do this, knowing the time, that now it is high time to awake out of sleep; for now our salvation is nearer than when we first believed (Romans 13:11 NKJV).

But you, beloved, building yourselves up on your most holy faith, praying in the Holy Spirit, keep yourselves in the love of God, looking for the mercy of our Lord Jesus Christ unto eternal life. And on some have compassion, making a distinction; but others save with fear, pulling them out of the fire, hating even the garment defiled by the flesh.

Now to Him who is able to keep you from stumbling, and to present you faultless before the presence of His glory with exceeding joy, To God our Savior, Who alone is wise, be glory and majesty, dominion and power, both now and forever. Amen (Jude 20-25 NKJV).

So, as I learned at 28, it remains as I have stepped into my 80s. I have read, and here, once more, urge you to do the same. I believe you'll be bettered for having read *The Fire That Never Sleeps.*

Yes, there is a Fire that never sleeps...and I believe you'll become more deeply aware, fully alert and adequately assisted to live in its warmth, light, and energy for having read the pages before you.

Let us go on!

PASTOR JACK HAYFORD
Chancellor and founder, The Kings University
President of International Church
of the Foursquare Gospel, 2004-2009
Founding Pastor, Church on the Way, Van Nuys CA

INTRODUCTION

DR. MICHAEL BROWN

As I taught on the subject of revival in the years leading up to Brownsville, I used definitions of revival that other leaders had coined, including things like, "Revival is God stepping down from Heaven," but I never came up with my own definition until teaching a class on revival at the Brownsville Revival School of Ministry. While not catchy, it does reflect my understanding of this critically important subject. Here's my working definition: "Revival is a season of unusual divine visitation resulting in deep repentance, supernatural renewal, and sweeping reformation in the Church, along with the radical conversion of sinners in the world, often producing moral, social, and even economic change in the local or national communities."

But what does revival look and feel like? Let me take you into a service from Brownsville so you can experience the sights and sounds of revival. Here's what I wrote in *The Revival Answer Book* (originally titled *Let No One Deceive You*). On Friday night, January 31, 1997, I returned from a service at the Brownsville Revival at

1:30 A.M. and was moved to write these words. They were written with an unusual urgency and intensity. No doubt you will sense it as you read.

I want to share my heart honestly with you, holding nothing back. I want to make myself totally vulnerable. The fact is, I *must*.

I have just come from the beautiful presence of the Lord, from a night of glorious baptismal testimonies and incredible stories of wonderfully changed lives; a night of sovereign visitation; a night of deep, sweeping repentance, of radical encounters with the living God, of public acts of repentance—from young people throwing their drugs and needles into the garbage to old people discarding their cigarettes; a night of weeping under conviction and rejoicing in newfound freedom; a night when the Spirit fell upon the children in a side room until their intercession and wailing permeated the sanctuary; a night when Jesus was exalted in the midst of His Church. Yes, I have come from the holy presence of the Lord at Brownsville Revival on January 31, 1997. The Spirit moved; the tears flowed; the Lord touched; the demons fled. This is what happens when revival is in the land!

At the end of the night, amid shouts of joy and victory, amid the sound of the newly redeemed enjoying their first moments free from captivity, I turned to my dear friend Evangelist Steve Hill and said, "We don't have to quote from the history books about revival. It's here! We're seeing it before our eyes."

Who can describe a night like this? Who can describe what it is like to be so caught up with God that Heaven is virtually here and you can almost sense the sound of the Judge knocking at the door? What can you say when young men come to the platform and begin to throw away their earrings, and another wants counsel because he doesn't know how to remove his *eyebrow* ring, and another tosses out his condoms, while another throws his knife into the trash? What can you say?

What can you say when a thousand people respond to the altar call and stay there for two hours getting right with God? What can you say when the prayers you have prayed for your nation, prayers for the real thing, for genuine visitation, for bona fide outpouring—not hype, not sensationalism, not a superficial show, but an awakening of historic proportions—when those prayers are being answered before your eyes and you know that your country will be *shaken*? What can you say?

What can you say when all you want is Jesus, when pleasing Him is your total delight, when you just have to tell everyone about God's great salvation, when sin's sweetest temptation is utterly repulsive to you, when you just can't find the words to express to the Lord how utterly wonderful He is, how He really is your all in all? What can you say at a sacred time like this? It is too precious to fully describe, too intimate to wholly communicate with mere human speech.

That was just one night in the midst of *years* of intense visitation, although, to be sure, it was an especially glorious night.

The problem, of course, is that it is not humanly possible to sustain something of such intensity over a long period of time, and even though the outpouring continued for the better part of five years, we were constantly thinking about long-term fruit. What happens to those in the revival today? Where will they be in five, or ten, or twenty years? And if God has given so much to us, how can we be good stewards and be sure that we pour back out what He has poured into us?

It was in that light that God gave me the vision to launch the Brownsville Revival School of Ministry in 1996, within weeks of getting involved in the revival myself, and it was a vision deeply affirmed by Pastor Kilpatrick, Steve Hill, and the other key leaders. We opened our doors in January 1997, and, by God's grace, now as FIRE School of Ministry, we continue to raise up and send out laborers to the nations.

Here's just a sampling of the some of the lasting fruit that came from the revival, evidenced in the lives of these ministry school graduates who are making a wonderful impact for Jesus around the globe. I wrote this on Saturday night, October 17, 2014, in the midst of our fifteenth annual missions conference at FIRE:

> We have all heard the bad news from the Middle East and have grieved over the onslaught of ISIS in Iraq and Syria. Well, the good news is that we have two families and several singles serving in northern Iraq, and in the midst of the chaos and upheaval, a powerful prayer movement has been birthed.
>
> Not only so, but as refugees have poured into the region, there has been an unprecedented openness to hear the Gospel.
>
> Sick bodies are being healed, lost sinners are being saved, and believers are being strengthened.
>
> We don't hear that in the nightly news.

You've also heard about the murderous rampage of Boko Haram in northern Nigeria.

One of our courageous, single female missionaries works with impoverished children, including Muslim children who are coming for education, some very near the Boko Haram territories. She is convinced that as the kids are educated they will be elevated, especially since they are receiving a biblical education, and that will be the best answer to radical Islam.

We heard reports from members of our large team in the Philippines. They are planting churches in rural, unreached regions, where the people only know traditional religion. They are caring for orphans, feeding needy children, starting discipleship training schools, and fighting against human trafficking. Recently, they were able to help a two-year-old girl whose mother had sold her into sex trafficking.

The stories go on and on.

Another grad showed a powerful video of Muslims coming to faith in large meetings he held in Pakistan.

We heard great reports about large youth rallies in Italy, where less than 1 percent of the native population is born-again. Doors have also opened in high schools for teams to share the Gospel, and the owner of a casino in Italy actually facilitated a Gospel outreach in front of his building. Jesus is Lord!

Some grads take multiday trips and hike for hours into the Andes Mountains in Peru to reach the lost, while others reach out to hopeless souls in a neglected town in England, and still others have been pelted with stones preaching the Gospel in Mexico.

Others reach out to the prostitutes in Tanzania, providing a home for them where they can be grounded in the Lord and kept safe. (That's just one of the many ministries our grads have birthed in Tanzania.)

Another grad just launched a FIRE School in Cameroon, and another opened one in Holland (the home of legalized prostitution, marijuana, same-sex "marriage," euthanasia, and much more), with other schools about to be birthed in other nations.

One grad has learned how to present the Gospel in culturally relevant cartoons that work for both the literate and illiterate. (In the past she worked with lepers in China and is now going to Southeast Asia.) Recently, a 103-year-old woman reading one of her cartoon books came to saving faith and now, at 104, loves to share the Gospel and worship.

Still other grads are taking orphans into their own homes and doing creative children's outreach where they can preach freely. One grad in India, together with her Indian husband, has started orphanages, children's schools, and ministry schools; planted churches; and conducted annual outreach services that draw as many as 60,000 Indians, the vast majority of them Hindus.

Some live and minister in the Buddhist world in countries like Thailand. Others labor in Japan, where large evangelical churches are almost unheard of, and still others start new works in Canada.

Our grads in Israel are involved in prayer movements, serving the poor and hurting, reaching out to nonbelieving Jews and Arabs and working toward reconciliation in the Messiah.

And then there are our faithful missionaries serving in parts of the Muslim world that we cannot disclose, as well as in other closed countries worldwide.

When one of our missionaries leaves his family each day, he says, "I'll see you tonight, or in Heaven," and he cannot stay in some major cities for more than twenty-four hours before the assassins are on his trail.

Another grad was martyred by Muslim terrorists (I cannot be specific for numerous reasons), and his widow (and the mother of their kids) continues to burn bright and do outreach here in America.

And speaking of America, where the needs are great as well, grads are making effective inroads into human trafficking in cities like Charlotte, North Carolina, with regular rescues, lots of proactive education, and the business community beginning to take a stand for righteousness.

Words fail me when I seek to describe what these precious men and women are doing, some with large families and others without; some in their seventies and others in their early twenties; some in the field now for more than fifteen years, many of them working among the poorest of the poor or taking the Gospel into the business world, all of them glorifying Jesus.

And I remind you: This is just a tiny sampling of the fruit that I know of firsthand. The great majority of fruit that the Brownsville Revival produced will only be counted in Heaven. It is vast, it is long-lasting, and it is powerful. Should we expect anything less?

INTRODUCTION

PASTOR JOHN KILPATRICK

Revival and resurrection are two different things. With a resurrection, there is *no* life. Someone is actually being raised from death to life. With revival, it's different. Resurrection is for the dead, but those who are still living need *revival*. They may be comatose and showing very faint signs of life. Their vitals might look very poor—even dismal. Their prognosis may be extremely negative, *but* if there is still any kind life, there is hope for revival. The same is true for the Church and the world today. The landscape may appear dark, but it's not dead. There is still *hope for revival*.

When we started praying for revival at Brownsville, I *knew* the Lord was going to do something. I was confident He was going to pour out His Spirit. He is faithful to respond to the hungry and He is trustworthy to answer the cries of His people. The Bible tells us this, time after time.

> *Let us know; let us press on to know the LORD; his*
> *going out is sure as the dawn; he will come to us as the*

showers, as the spring rains that water the earth (Hosea 6:3).

"Ask, and it will be given to you; seek, and you will find; knock, and it will be opened to you" (Matthew 7:7).

He will surely be gracious to you at the sound of your cry. As soon as he hears it, he answers you (Isaiah 30:19).

You will seek me and find me when you seek me with all your heart (Jeremiah 29:13).

Historically God has answered the desperate cries of His people. This is what caused me to be filled with expectation as our church family at Brownsville Assembly of God cried out for revival. In fact, the Lord told me that as we made His house a *house of prayer*, He would pour out His Spirit in a powerful way. This is exactly what happened.

What took place on Father's Day—June 18, 1995—*exceeded* my expectations. Yes, He is the God who answers prayers. At the same time, He is also the God of Ephesians 3:20, "who is able to do immeasurably more than all we ask or imagine" (NIV). Revival is truly an over-answer to prayer.

Over the years, I had spent a considerable amount of time studying the great past revivals and revivalists. Even back then, I would have identified as a student of revival. Though I studied the great moves of God, I never thought I would get to participate in such a historic outpouring of the Spirit. I had no idea that what our church community was praying for would be fulfilled in such a large way.

When I thought of *revival*, my limited imagination conceived of maybe six, seven, or eight weeks of meetings where people were saved, delivered, and baptized in the Holy Spirit. I had no idea that it would last for five years. I had no idea that what happened in our midst at Brownsville would have such far-reaching implications. I had *no* idea that to this day, men and women would be powerfully advancing the Kingdom of God all across the world because the fires of revival touched them in Pensacola, Florida, from 1995 to 2000. I had one idea of what revival looked like; God clearly had another.

In view of how God moved at Brownsville, I invite you to do everything you know how to do in seeking revival. Are you hungry for the move of His Spirit? Then cry out. Pray. Ask…and keep asking. He *will* respond; but know that the God who responds to the cries of His people is also the God of more than enough. He wants to over-answer your prayers, too.

Up until revival broke out, I had a completely different paradigm of what church should look like. Everything changed because the Holy Spirit powerfully introduced us to His agenda—His order for church. After revival, I was ruined for "church as usual," based on the way things had always been done. Revival reintroduces church not according to man's protocol, but to God's presence.

I also discovered that John Wesley's words are profoundly true: When you catch on fire, people will come to watch you burn. In our case, it was an entire church community that caught on fire. As a result, the nations came to see what was happening. This was completely beyond anything I could have imagined.

I saw people hungry and desperate for God unlike I had ever seen before.

I saw spiritual hunger among different races, nationalities, and ethnicities.

I saw sinners—people who did *not* even know Jesus—show up outside the church, waiting in long lines for the doors to open.

I saw airplanes landing at our small local airport, unloading people from all over the world who were desperate to be touched by God.

People with no spiritual background whatsoever were streaming to the revival. How could this be? Jesus's timeless words bring everything into perspective: "And when I am lifted up from the earth, I will draw everyone to myself" (John 12:32 NLT).

As the Holy Spirit illuminated this Scripture to my heart, what was happening in our midst started to make more sense. As Jesus was being exalted in the worship, in testimony, and in preaching, the Spirit of God was drawing saints and sinners alike to that place. For burnt out, weary, and backslidden believers, the Holy Spirit brought a great refreshing. For those lost in sin, addiction, and bondage, the Spirit brought mighty salvation and deliverance.

We did not need to advertise or promote the revival. This was long before the era of social media and live-streaming. At the time, the Internet was still new. Even though we didn't have access to all the media options available today, word still got around and millions came. I discovered that you don't need television, marketing, Internet, or news media to attract people when the Holy Spirit is truly moving in power. His presence and fire are enough.

In this book, I trust that the Holy Spirit will set your heart ablaze, for it is the Spirit alone who can make a heart burn for revival. Only the Holy Spirit can cause your heart to yearn for revival, and, likewise, it is only the Spirit who can satisfy such a deep yearning.

The pages you are about to read are purposed to ignite your heart to burn for revival, for it is revival that is the answer to the ills of the Church and the world. There is still hope for a landscape-changing move of God's Spirit. Remember, where there is still life, there is the possibility of revival.

We must work the works of him who sent me while it is day; night is coming, when no one can work (John 9:4).

Let's burn brightly while it is still day so others can catch this fire, and revival will transition into a national awakening. This is truly what happens when the *fire never sleeps.*

CHAPTER 1

THE FIRE THAT NEVER SLEEPS

LARRY SPARKS

God is a consuming fire.
The Holy Spirit is a Spirit of fire.
And Jesus said, "I've come to bring fire on earth."
There is no escaping fire.
—LEONARD RAVENHILL

God is looking for a people who will keep His fire burning upon the altar of their hearts.

Such a people are not satisfied with an intense spiritual experience or an emotional moment; they desire to walk a sustained lifestyle of personal revival.

This is exactly why we have all come together to present you with this book. Dr. Michael Brown and Pastor John Kilpatrick were key leaders in one of the greatest moves of God to ever grace North America—the Brownsville Revival. From 1995 to 2000, Brownsville Assembly of God in Pensacola, Florida, was a center for spiritual renewal that attracted pilgrims from across the earth.

> When we decide that *true revival* is what takes place outside the four walls of a church or meeting center, we are one step closer to sustaining a lifestyle of passion and zeal for Jesus.

During the course of the revival, roughly 4.5 million people from around the world converged upon Pensacola to attend the revival services at Brownsville Assembly of God. It is also estimated that hundreds of thousands of people responded to the altar calls and either gave their hearts to Christ for the first time or rededicated their lives to Jesus. The outstanding number of conversions, by itself, marks this revival as a most significant spiritual movement. That's not it, though. While thousands came to Christ, countless others came *back* to Christ. Their fire for God was reignited. As a result, Brownsville launched a missionary movement that is still impacting nations across the earth today. The leaders were not content to contain the revival or even to keep it restricted to the southeast United States.

In response to this historic move of God, a school was birthed that continues to carry the fire of God to the nations today. The Brownsville Revival School of Ministry—now Fire School of Ministry—ensured that the fire of God did not remain in one geographic place. When fire spreads, it can't sleep. When we decide that *true revival* is what takes place outside the four walls of a church or meeting center, we are one step closer to sustaining a lifestyle of passion and zeal for Jesus.

A VISION FOR A REVIVED LIFESTYLE

Throughout the pages to come, we are not simply recounting stories about what God did *back then* during Brownsville. That would be easy. While such an approach might get people excited and provide some nostalgia about "the good old days," it keeps us distant from the potential of the present. Revival is not something that happened in the 1800s during the Great Awakenings, or in the early 1900s with the Azusa Street Revival, or even in the 1990s during the Brownsville Revival or Toronto Blessing. What we define as *revival* is God's pattern for normal Christianity. We *will* be sharing stories and testimonies, but with purpose. They are intended to give you a clear vision of what revival should ignite in our lives.

Rather than just memorializing a movement, we are presenting a vision for what a lifestyle of *sustained personal revival* looks like. More than anything, we want to give you a practical plan for how you can live on fire for God when your world, your surroundings, your environment, your job, your school, your community, your family, and maybe even your church are not encouraging your walk with Him. Truth be told, regardless of where everyone else is in their pursuit of God, your relationship with Him is your responsibility. I have heard it said that you are as close to God as you want to be. Likewise, you are as revived as you want to be.

THE DAYS WE ARE LIVING IN

We certainly live in dark days. It doesn't take prophetic eyesight to see that evil appears to be prevailing in the world around us.

While some observe this darkness as a summons to hopelessness and defeat, we look to the assuring promises of Scripture:

> *Arise, shine, for your light has come, and the glory of the Lord has risen upon you. For behold, darkness shall cover the earth, and thick darkness the peoples; but the Lord will arise upon you, and his glory will be seen upon you. And nations shall come to your light, and kings to the brightness of your rising* (Isaiah 60:1-3).

Events come and go, but a people who keep the fire of God burning on the altar of their hearts actually *carry* this fire within them...wherever they go.

This is not your time to retreat; it is your time to *arise and shine*! How will this *arising* take place? Simple—when Christians decide that revival should *not* be limited to a special church service, meeting, or certain flavor of spirituality. Revival as an event will *not* suffice anymore. Events come and go, but a people who keep the fire of God burning on the altar of their hearts actually *carry* this fire within them...wherever they go. At this point, the fire becomes transferrable.

RELEASING BURNING ONES

As wonderful as revival meetings, services, conferences, and events are, they all exist for a purpose. Services are never the end goal; transformation is. Meetings and events are means to accomplish an end, and the end is you carrying the power and presence of God into your unique sphere of influence, *wherever* that may be.

God is looking to release His burning ones into every arena of society—not to overthrow, but to serve as His ambassadors.

The key word is *release.*

> **When the presence of God divinely visits a specific location, it is for the purpose of making a deposit. He wants to expose people to a glimpse of what normal looks like.**

Revival remains contained when it stays within the context of a local church. As much as we desire—and need—revived churches, the end vision for revival should not be more people sitting in buildings but rather more people serving in the "streets" of society. Again, these "streets" represent wherever God has placed you: the business world, education, the medical profession, the arts, media, government, politics, law, entertainment, and, most important, your own household and family. We want to see the fire of God leave a measurable mark on how we do life. The ultimate evaluation of whether revival was a "success" has little to do with how long church services or meetings continue uninterrupted in one region or venue for a certain period of time. This is actually a small part of revival. Yes, sooner or later the meetings die down and the church services go from every night, to three times a week, to back to normal. Never let these factors determine whether revival was a success. Find the people who were present during the Brownsville Revival and ask them about the life changes they experienced—and are still experiencing to this very day. When the presence of God divinely visits a specific location, it is for the purpose of making a deposit. He wants to expose people to a glimpse of what normal looks like.

No, normal is not sustained church services; it is most clearly represented by the lives of those who came into revival one way and left another. Normal is sustained, continuous transformation into the image of Christ, from glory to glory (see 2 Cor. 3:18). Normal is not perfection; it's pursuit. Normal is living your everyday life under the influence of the Holy Spirit. Normal is saying yes to God in every season and situation, no matter what He asks. Normal is praying for the sick and tormented, and believing that the same power that raised Jesus from the dead lives inside you—and is able to bring wholeness to the afflicted. Normal is going against the rising tide of culture and yielding to the conviction of the Holy Spirit.

> Awakening is not out with the old and in with the new; it's out with the dry, stale, formal way of "doing church" and *in* with the normal expression of Christianity as revealed in the Book of Acts.

Revival is all about escorting us out of religion, dryness, and spiritual lethargy, and ushering us into "normal" as defined by Jesus.

Revival is about stewarding the deposit of divine visitation. When God comes, it's not for the sake of hype and excitement. He comes to show us what life *really is.*

Revival is actually living out what we see pictured in Leviticus 6:12—"The fire on the altar shall be kept burning on it; it shall not go out." God made the ultimate deposit in His people when He gave us the Holy Spirit at Pentecost. The great question is: *What will we do with His Spirit and fire within us?*

BE THE OUTPOURING

We need something fresh in the Church today. We can't continue on with business as usual. Many talk of renewal, revival, and outpouring. The question is *where is this nation-shaking move of God going to come from?* Are we waiting for something new to come down out from Heaven, or are we pressing in for a great awakening of global proportion?

> **We don't need another Holy Spirit; we need to yield our lives to the One who already lives within us.**

Awakening is not out with the old and in with the new; it's out with the dry, stale, formal way of "doing church" and *in* with the normal expression of Christianity as revealed in the Book of Acts. It's time to carefully evaluate what we—in our sophisticated twenty-first century world—have embraced as the "normal Christian life," and to measure it beside the timeless standards of Jesus, His disciples, and the early Church. Methods change over time, but the message cannot be compromised. They did not employ the latest gimmicks to entice prospective followers; nor did they have technology that arrested both the eyes and ears in some kind of visceral experience. Their source of power and effectiveness was in the very person of the Holy Spirit. Even with everything we have access to in contemporary Christianity, we must ask the question: Are we drawing from the endless supernatural well of the Holy Spirit, or are we trying to manufacture an experience using our own methods? At the day's end, *nothing man creates can compare to or substitute for the Spirit's presence in our midst.*

Here is the glorious news: God has already sent the Holy Spirit to us, which means that Act 2 is still sufficient for us today! The person and power of Pentecost is our great inheritance! We don't need an upgraded Holy Spirit. In Romans 8:11, Paul makes it clear that "the Spirit of him who raised Jesus from the dead dwells in you." This statement never fails to fill me with awe for the One who has made our hearts His dwelling place. We don't need another Holy Spirit; we need to yield our lives to the One who already lives within us. *This is awakening.* Too many Christians are waiting for some kind of new spiritual experience, when instead we need to rediscover how to steward what we have already received.

In and of themselves, experiences are not bad—in fact, they are quite necessary. They often jump-start us. They awaken us to the higher reality of the Christian life. Usually it is through our experiences with God that our eyes are opened to what we were missing *before* the experience. In a moment, we are able to measure the mediocrity of our present Christian life beside a mere touch of God's glory and power. It's amazing how just a glimpse of the authentic stirs a desire within us to completely abandon the mediocre. The key is learning how to *always* set the Lord before us, just as David wrote in Psalm 16:8.

> *I have set the Lord always before me; because he is at my right hand, I shall not be shaken.*

David had many life-changing encounters with God. His personal history is absolutely filled with incredible miracles and testimonies of the Lord's mighty power. And yet this shepherd/king—the man after God's own heart—did not wait around for another experience before He sought God. In his joy, in his pain, in his sorrow, and in his confusion, Scripture shows us a man who decided to set the Lord *always* before Him.

In short, David was a man who said yes to God. Even when he fell into grievous sin, he said yes to God through repentance.

REVIVAL STARTS WITH YOUR "YES"

Just like David, we celebrate the landmark moments in our spiritual histories. We must, as they are essential and catalytic. They take us from one level to the next. It is no coincidence that Paul describes the process as moving from *glory to glory* in Second Corinthians 3:18. True revival is profoundly glorious because it possesses the capacity to take people—be it an individual, a church, or even an entire community—from one level of the Christian experience to another.

There have been many definitions assigned to *revival* over the years. For the sake of our journey here, I want us to think of it in terms of a reintroduction to normal. This is exactly how Dr. Michael Brown and Pastor John Kilpatrick observe it. Dr. Brown described revival as "a season of unusual divine visitation resulting in deep repentance, supernatural renewal, and sweeping reformation in the Church, along with the radical conversion of sinners in the world, often producing moral, social, and even economic change in the local or national communities." Pastor Kilpatrick explains that revival is "not church as usual." In fact, revival exchanges the old "usual" for a new "usual." When revival comes, some of what accompanies it would be considered "abnormal" or "unusual." Why? It's been so long since these things were *usual* in the Church and in our lives that we have labeled them as unusual. By God's grace, the unusual is starting to become usual again!

A few things that revival is *not*:

Revival is *not* a series of special meetings at church.

Revival is *not* what a church does a few times a year to simply draw in new converts (although we celebrate true conversions when they take place).

Revival is *not* about the unusual, physical manifestations that tend to happen when people are "touched by the Holy Spirit."

Great Christian author A. W. Tozer made this most relevant observation about praying for revival: "Have you noticed how much praying for revival has been going on of late—and how little revival has resulted? I believe the problem is that we have been trying to substitute praying for obeying, and it simply will not work."

Yes, this book is designed to stir your passion to pray for revival. In fact, our hope is that your prayers for revival become richer, most impassioned, and deeper than ever before. But perhaps even more, our vision is to help you position yourself to *become* the revival that the Church is praying for and that this world so desperately needs. For us to become an expression of revival on the earth, we must say an unqualified yes to everything Jesus requires from us. That's it, right there—the key to living a lifestyle of sustained, personal revival. It all begins with our willingness to say yes to anything and everything the Lord asks of us. It's about saying yes to His word, His ways, and His direction. In view of who God is, how could we offer up any other response?

For some, praying for revival has become one prayer request among many others. We pray for revival in the church and then we go on to pray for our friends who have lost their jobs. Revival is not something we can take or leave. A day is coming when four songs, a sermon, and an offering simply will not work anymore. Perhaps this model has been functional for a season, but in an hour of deep darkness, we need to be a people who carry the light of the Kingdom. This will only happen as Christians live *revival lifestyles*.

In the pages ahead, you will catch a vision of what true revival looks like. I am also convinced that the anointed reflections and powerful testimonies will awaken within you a desperate hunger *for* revival. Yes, you keep praying—but such prayer is not passive. It is obedient. It contends. It cries out. It is not about strong-arming God into doing something or manipulating Him into sending some new outpouring. The Holy Spirit is here. Now it's time to give this precious One the ultimate "yes" in every area of your life.

Prayer for revival starts with being so gripped by Heaven's vision of the Christian life that everything you have embraced as normal becomes unacceptable, and you start pressing in for everything Jesus made available to you.

Open your heart.

Be expectant.

You aren't just reading words; I am confident you are receiving an impartation.

Get ready to take your place as one who keeps the fire burning!

PART ONE

OUR PRESENT CONDITION

DR. MICHAEL BROWN

Where are we as a church? What shape are we in as the saints of God? Are we fulfilling the Great Commission and drawing from the rich well of our spiritual inheritance in Christ, or are we settling for a substandard redefinition of Christianity that has been polluted and compromised by popular culture?

Revival is not "out with the old and in with the new." I've heard it said that it's "out with the old and in with the even older." To experience revival, we need to recognize the difference between what was considered normal for Jesus and His followers and where we are today.

Only when we honestly confront our present condition can we truly cry out for holy visitation and divine transformation. This cry is awakened as we simply discover that where we currently *are* is *not* what God has made available to us.

There is more!

> *Today, we have a Christianity made easy as an*
> *accommodation to an age that is unwilling to face*
> *the implication of Calvary, and the gospel of "simply*
> *believism" has produced a harvest of professions which*
> *have done untold harm to the cause of Christ.*
> —DUNCAN CAMPBELL

> *Do you have a hunger for God? If we don't feel*
> *strong desires for the manifestation of the glory of*
> *God, it is not because we have drunk deeply and*
> *are satisfied. It is because we have nibbled so long*
> *at the table of the world. Our soul is stuffed with*
> *small things, and there is no room for the great.*
> —JOHN PIPER

> *The world has lost the power to blush over its vice;*
> *the Church has lost her power to weep over it.*
> —LEONARD RAVENHILL

CHAPTER 2

WHO CHANGED THINGS?

*There is exceedingly much difference
between what ought be and what is.*
—CHARLES SPURGEON

W ho changed things from the vibrant, Spirit-empowered "by life or by death" faith of the New Testament to today's spineless home-and-garden Sunday-morning religion?

Who changed things from "Leave everything and follow Me" (see Luke 14:33) to "Pray this little prayer and you're set for eternity"?

Who changed things from "All who live godly lives in Christ Jesus will suffer persecution" (see 2 Tim. 3:12) to "Ask Jesus into your heart and enjoy a comfortable life"?

Who changed things from a fearless proclamation of the truth, whatever the cost or consequences, to a watered-down, compromised message that is afraid to offend anyone?

By what authority, by whose decree, based on what new revelation have we so blatantly departed from the faith of the apostles? Who changed things?

Who changed things from the New Testament faith, where even the disciples couldn't minister without the Spirit's enduement, to today's version, where whole ministries are run with hardly any evidence of the Spirit's work?

As A.W. Tozer once said,

> "If the Holy Spirit was withdrawn from the church today, 95 percent of what we do would go on and no one would know the difference. If the Holy Spirit had been withdrawn from the New Testament church, 95 percent of what they did would stop, and everybody would know the difference."

This remains true of most of the contemporary church in the West.

Who changed things from a God-centered faith to a man-centered faith, from "Take up your cross and deny yourself" to "Bypass the cross and empower yourself"?

Who changed things from holiness being beautiful to holiness being bondage, and from the early Church being known for its high standards to the contemporary Church being known for its scandals?

Who changed things from the people of God being a threat to the powers of darkness to the people of God being active participants in darkness?

In the early church, Paul instructed the Corinthians to separate themselves from people who claimed to be believers but were living in outward, unrepentant sin (see 1 Cor. 5). Today, some of those people lead our churches and preach from our pulpits. Who changed things?

Who changed things from a faith that was so focused on the life of Jesus and so infused with the reality of His death and resurrection that no sacrifice was considered too great and no act of service too extreme—to the contrary, suffering for Him was considered a privilege (see Matt. 5:10-12, Acts 5:41, Phil. 1:29)—to today's convenience-store Christianity, where we have to "sell" salvation to the sinner by spicing up the deal with perks and benefits?

When did Jesus stop being enough?

When did obedience become an option?

When did keeping God's commandments out of love for Him become "religious" (in the negative sense of the word)? Didn't Jesus say that if we loved Him, we would keep His commandments (see John 14:15, 21)?

Who changed things?

If we belonged to another religion that claimed to have other books that supplemented the Bible or traditions that superseded it, that would be one thing.

But we don't. We believe the Scriptures alone are God's Word and that nothing that comes after the Scriptures—no tradition, no alleged revelation, no consensus—can undermine or countermand the written Word of God.

So who changed things from the biblical version of the Jesus faith to the modern American version?

We can debate church history and blame this group or that group, and we can point out what's wrong with this denomination and that denomination. We might even have some great historical and contemporary insights.

But unless we get back to believing what is written and acting on what is written, we will continue to perpetuate our merry-go-round Christianity with lots of noise and action and bells and whistles but with little authority, little purity, and little effect (if any).

I didn't get the memo that God's Word and Spirit were not enough, and I'm far more concerned with what He says than with what the latest polls say.

Really, now, since when did the Lord command us to fashion our preaching and our style of worship and even the way we look based on what's trending?

If some church leaders choose to trust in worldly business models and carnal consulting firms, that's their choice. I say we go with the power of the name of Jesus and the wisdom of the Word of God and the fullness of the Spirit. I say we go with the New Testament model, applied with boldness and compassion to the needs of the day.

Years ago, Leonard Ravenhill said, "One of these days some simple soul will pick up the Book of God, read it, and believe it. Then the rest of us will be embarrassed."

I want to be that simple soul. How about you?

CHAPTER 3

IT'S TIME

We must wake ourselves up!
Or somebody else will take our
place, and bear our cross,
and thereby rob us of our crown.
—WILLIAM BOOTH

I refuse to believe that what we see in churches across America is what God planned for His people. I refuse to believe that it is the God-intended norm.

The Word of God is against it.

Church history is against it.

What the Spirit is doing around the world is against it.

What I have experienced in my own life is against it.

Everything inside me is shouting, "There must be more! We must go deeper!"

Is that same voice shouting inside you?

> Take hold of everything He has promised and everything He has called us to, and, by His grace, pursue and obey Him until His reality becomes our reality.

THERE MUST BE MORE

If the death and resurrection of Jesus are real—and they are—there must be more. If the outpouring of the Spirit is real—and it is—there must be more. If the promises of God are real—and they are—there must be more. If the requirements of the Lord are real—and they are—there must be more.

It's high time we quit trying to drag the Word of God down to our level of experience and commitment, trying to conform Scripture to our ways rather than conforming our ways to Scripture. Instead, we need to take hold of everything He has promised and everything He has called us to, and, by His grace, pursue and obey Him until His reality becomes our reality.

WHAT'S NORMAL ANYMORE?

What does God's reality look like? What is normal according to the word? As I have said for many years, what the world calls fanaticism and most of the church calls extremism, God calls normal. In the words of Leonard Ravenhill, "Christianity today is so subnormal that if any Christian began to act like a normal New Testament Christian, he would be considered abnormal."

What does normal look like, according to Jesus?

Whoever loves father or mother more than me is not worthy of me, and whoever loves son or daughter more than me is not worthy of me. And whoever does not take his cross and follow me is not worthy of me. Whoever finds his life will lose it, and whoever loses his life for my sake will find it (Matthew 10:37-39).

What does normal look like, according to Paul? (Let's remember that Paul told us to follow his example; see 1 Cor. 11:1, Phil. 4:9.)

It is my eager expectation and hope that I will not be at all ashamed, but that with full courage now as always Christ will be honored in my body, whether by life or by death. For to me to live is Christ, and to die is gain (Philippians 1:20-21).

Unfortunately, as expressed by Watchman Nee, "By the time the average Christian gets his temperature up to normal, everybody thinks he has a fever."

I say it's time we burn. In fact, the Word commands us to be fervent (which means red-hot) in spirit in Romans 12:11, so that others can catch fire as well.

They can call us crazy, judge us as religious extremists, and put us out of their company. But if we walk in humility, if we bless and don't curse, if we honor those in authority while determining to obey the Lord no matter what, the fruit of our lives will be the proof of God's goodness. And people will come flocking to us, saying, "I need what you have. How can I experience more of God in my life?"

WHAT IS REVIVAL?

In my introduction to this book, I gave a working definition of revival, but I want to return to that subject from a different angle to be sure we have a clear understanding.

When you hear the word *revival*, what images come to mind? Some people just think of a series of special meetings, as in "We are holding a revival at our church next month." Some people think in terms of emotionalism—it's just a matter of a bunch of people getting worked up or some kind of silly charismatic display.

A revived church must, in turn, impact the world.

Others recognize that we are talking about Divine visitation. They understand that we are talking about God coming in such a way that the measure of His activity and presence in our midst can have an earth-shattering effect, even on the culture.

I define revival as a season of *unusual* Divine visitation. Remember, God is always present with His people on some level. The Holy Spirit lives within every believer. He is present in His Church. On a greater scale, He is omnipresent. But there are times of unusual Divine visitation, and they come with deep, massive conviction of sin. They come with supernatural repentance and renewal. They come with a return of backsliders, the conversion of lost sinners, and the refreshing of the saints. Revival causes God's people to start living like God's people and worldly people to come to faith. The impact is so significant that it has an effect on the culture that can be absolutely revolutionary in size and scope.

Revival is not an end in itself. While I celebrate the visitation of God's Spirit in our midst wherever it happens, my heart burns to see the by-product of revival: cultural revolution. A revived church must, in turn, impact the world. Otherwise we are quite correct in questioning the "fruit" of revival.

Did the outpouring of the Spirit create an outpouring of love and of evangelism? Was the visitation responded to in such a way that those who were touched in a meeting *left* that meeting lastingly changed?

The amazing thing is that God can touch anyone, from any background. I saw this night after night as the lost—often living completely godless lifestyles—were noticeably touched by the presence of God during the Brownsville Revival. Their response to God's movement upon their lives is what ensured their transformation.

Oh, that the body of Christ in this hour would receive such a touch from the Spirit that it produces a transformation in our world! *This* is how revival affects change outside the four walls of the church building. *This* is how revival is the supernatural solution to the many ills we are presently confronting in society.

Revival introduces us to the *better* taste of God's presence.

As I said many years ago, the more drug dealers are saved, the more drug dealing diminishes. This is simply a by-product of that sinful culture being infiltrated by the in-breaking of God's Spirit. Now, take that thought process and apply it on a societal level. Revival touches individuals, and those transformed individuals in turn change the climate of their spheres of influence.

Study the history of revival, and you will see examples of entire communities where sin became sparse because of God's renewing movement upon His people. It all begins when God's people start living as God's people. This is the catalyst for transformation.

If believers in America quit watching pornography and sexually explicit movies on TV and the Internet, the industry would take a massive hit overnight. Revival sanctifies our pleasure. When we look to the world for pleasure, we are living out of deception, and one main reason we do not live holy lives is because we have not tasted something *better* than what the world offers. Revival introduces us to the *better* taste of God's presence. When He becomes our great pursuit, by default, anything that does not reflect Him or honor Him will be stripped out of our lives; we simply will not tolerate it.

Just think about it. If revived Christians lived holy lives, completely dedicated and sold out to Jesus, the industries peddling immorality would go into decline. Take it a step further. When worldly people start being saved, sinful industries not only suffer, they are often infiltrated and transformed.

OUR FITTING RESPONSE

Missionary C. T. Studd once said, "If Jesus Christ be God, and died for me, then no sacrifice can be too great for me to make for Him." This is the reality we must live by.

The glorious Son of God shed His blood on our behalf, dying for our sins so we could belong to God, bringing us into His family as brothers and sisters. His Father is now our Father, and we are joint heirs with Him. (See Romans 8:14-17.) This is the truth that we are responding to with our lives. Such divine love demands nothing less than *everything*.

The key is ever setting these facts before our gaze. When we forget what the true New Testament faith looks like and what it should be built upon, our response weakens. Our devotion wanes cold. Passion comes and goes. Suddenly our faith becomes expressed through a weekly event, not a moment-to-moment lifestyle.

Studd summons us back to the wondrous cross and the radical call of that cross. And yet when we give our everything to follow the Savior, He in turns gives everything to empower us for the journey ahead.

Consider the words of Paul: "He who did not spare his own Son but gave him up for us all, how will he not also with him graciously give us all things?" (Rom. 8:32). All things!

That is the glorious Gospel. How should we respond?

Jesus says, "Follow me"—and that means all that we have, all that we are, and all that we ever could be belongs to Him. We now live to do His will, with our eyes set on Him, and our life goal is to know Him and make Him known, regardless of cost or consequence.

That is normal, according to the New Testament.

"FOLLOW ME..."

As Paul wrote in Second Corinthians, Jesus died for all so that "those who live might no longer live for themselves but for him who for their sake died and was raised" (2 Cor. 5:15).

Or, as he said to the Colossians, "If then you have been raised with Christ, seek the things that are above, where Christ is, seated at the right hand of God. Set your minds on things that are above, not on things that are on earth. For you have died, and your life is hidden with Christ in God" (Col. 3:1-3).

Or, as expressed by Peter, we are to live "for the rest of the time in the flesh no longer for human passions but for the will of God" (1 Pet. 4:2).

This is beautiful, not binding—our act of gratitude as recipients of grace, not our futile effort to receive His grace. And because of that grace and mercy, we belong totally to Him: "Therefore," Paul writes, "I exhort you, brothers and sisters, by the mercies of God, to present your bodies as a sacrifice—alive, holy, and pleasing to God—which is your reasonable service" (or "your spiritual worship") (Rom. 12: NET).

So let us crucify every distraction; let us count ourselves dead to sin and alive to God; let us ask the Spirit to work afresh in our lives; and let us take hold of the challenge that fueled the fires of D. L. Moody's life, as spoken to him by revivalist Henry Varley: "Moody, the world has yet to see what God will do with a man fully consecrated to him."

Isn't it time that our nations see what God will do with a man or woman fully consecrated to Him? Isn't it time that our generation has a true demonstration of the Gospel? This is normal, not abnormal, and so I encourage you to join me in striving to be normal in the Lord's sight, by the grace and power of God.

It's time.

CHAPTER 4

THE STATE OF THE CHURCH

*The chief danger of the Church today is that it is
trying to get on the same side as the world, instead of
turning the world upside down. Our Master expects us
to accomplish results, even if they bring opposition and
conflict. Anything is better than compromise, apathy,
and paralysis. God give to us an intense cry for the
old-time power of the Gospel and the Holy Ghost!*
—A. B. Simpson

In many ways in the American Church, we have settled for a
substandard view of what true Gospel faith really is. As our understanding of the faith has become skewed, so has our expression of
what a life yielded to Christ looks like.

That's another reason why revival is our most desperate need in
this hour—not because we crave something new, but because we

desire to recapture something ancient, something pure. In order to walk in a New Testament demonstration of the Gospel, we must model the lifestyles of those who were part of the early Church community. I pray that these pages will sound the alarm for you, as there is *so much more* to life in Jesus than most of us are presently experiencing.

IT DIDN'T HAPPEN OVERNIGHT

We did not get into our present condition overnight, just as we don't grow old or gain 100 pounds overnight. It's been gradual. On the one hand, we have watered down our message more and more over the years. We have preached less about a God to whom we are accountable. We have moved away from any message that would make people uncomfortable. We have watered down the Gospel in our preaching and teaching. We haven't been willing to confront sin. Where we have confronted sin, we've done it in a political way more than a spiritual way. We have let our own standards drop. We have left our first love.

We have also allowed for the deterioration of marriage and family within the Church. This is the result of not recognizing the onslaught of culture and the infiltration of such things as sexual temptation through pornography, the power of materialism through greed, and the power of worldly seduction through entertainment.

Instead of recognizing how powerful these sinful influences are and what we need to do to be vigilant in our walk with God—to be more comfortable with Him than we are with the world—we've just allowed the flood of the world to enter our midst. Christians no longer become agents of change; instead we are the ones who are undergoing the change. The world is actually evangelizing the church. This has been a long, methodical process, but even now, we see the results in a community of professing believers who, in many ways, resemble the very system they are called to transform.

Sadly, we have adopted a theology of cultural relevance. We think the only way we can win the world is by becoming like the world, rather than recognizing the only way we can win the world is by becoming like Jesus.

In truth, there are multiple external forces aimed at believers today. We live in a generation and culture that has seen a rise in aggressive atheism. Anti-fundamentalism has emerged, as if committed Christians can be compared to the Taliban or the 9/11 bombers and somehow make up this radical, dangerous group— not dangerous in a Gospel sense, but in a destructive sense. And many Christians now don't want to be identified with Christianity or the Bible, and they try to package things in a different way that avoids the stumbling block of the cross. The ultimate result of all these factors is that we end up becoming just like the world we have been sent to impact.

TWO KINDS OF CHRISTIANITY

We know very little about the pure Gospel today. We share our testimonies with our friends and coworkers. We get people to pray the sinner's prayer, and then we bring them to our discipleship classes. But so many times we fail to see real conversion, deep transformation, and genuine salvation. How many people are pursuing us—their hearts shattered with conviction, their self-confidence utterly destroyed, their absolute need totally apparent—with a cry of, "Save me or I perish!" on their lips?

One reason that the scene I just described is rare to nonexistent in the Western world is because our current demonstration of the faith betrays the lifestyle that Jesus has called us into. For many, a new kind of Christianity has emerged that is becoming increasingly compatible with sin, unrighteousness, and the world's system. At its core, the message is nothing more than a gimmicky formula to attain success and live the "good life" in this world.

Does God promise to bless us? Yes. Does He provide for us, heal our bodies, and grant us the *abundant life* as described by Jesus in John 10:10? Absolutely. Unfortunately we have completely redefined what this abundant life is and what it looks like to walk it out. In many places, following Jesus is not about taking up His cross and living for Him; rather it is using biblical principles almost like a vending machine to get what we want out of God. It basically makes the church into a glorified self-help club, and, at its essence, this is *another Gospel*, a completely disfigured version of the Gospel faith. It is abnormal, and thus skews our understanding of what normal looks like.

THE TWO CROSSES

Many years ago, A. W. Tozer said that whereas the old cross killed the sinner, the new cross redirects the sinner. Consider his timely words:

> The new cross does not slay the sinner, it redirects him. It gears him into a cleaner and jollier way of living and saves his self-respect. To the self-assertive it says, "Come and assert yourself for Christ." To the egotist it says, "Come and do your boasting in the Lord." To the thrill seeker it says, "Come and enjoy the thrill of Christian fellowship." The Christian message is slanted in the direction of the current vogue in order to make it acceptable to the public.

It would seem that in twenty-first century Christianity, there are two crosses—the authentic and the counterfeit. The authentic cross calls us to surrender all while the counterfeit pats us on the back and assures us that we can take the world along for the journey.

This is why true, sustained revival continues to evade us. We are becoming like the system we have been commissioned to transform. In compromising with the world by embracing *another cross*, we offer a great disservice to the very people who are desperately in need of God.

If we use the world to draw the world in, ultimately we will try to use the world to keep them in.

We try to offer them a Christianized, repackaged version of the world, hoping that our relevant "tools of evangelism" are effective in deceiving them into the Kingdom. We are dressing up our strategies with so much worldliness that when people actually respond to them, we must maintain this compromised climate in the houses of worship we are luring them to. This is why so many churches are looking more and more like the world.

This is not an affront on contemporary music or a rejection of relevant tools to help connect a new generation with the Gospel. These are important methods if we are going to properly steward our message in the context we have been placed in. The means can and must change to suit the culture, generation, and context, but the message cannot.

If we use the world to draw the world in, ultimately we will try to use the world to keep them in. Here is the question: Who is ultimately being transformed, the church or the world? These are not words of condemnation—they are a clear call of hope. Let's reject this temptation to compromise and instead *be the Church that Jesus defined.*

THE TIMELESS CALL OF CALVARY

Tozer spoke of two crosses: the old and the new. As we all know, there is only one *true cross*. Unfortunately the invitation of Calvary is often not seen as attractive and thus needs to be redefined for a more "modern generation."

The cross of old calls us to lay everything before Jesus and completely turn our lives over to Him rather than simply asking God to bless our best efforts and intentions. If we want to walk out lifestyles of sustained revival, this cannot be an acceptable expression of the faith. Many are the prayers for supernatural power and miraculous demonstrations, but few are the cries of repentance and surrender.

The cross is not some addition to our lives; it demands our complete redefinition. Our pursuits and passions become aligned with Heaven's. Our focus is no longer selfish and self-seeking; it becomes thoroughly God-centric. In many places today, the cross is not a call to die to our old sinful nature, but rather an all-access pass to do our thing and be infinitely blessed. After all, everything was taken care of on the cross. To believe such a statement proves that we have little grasp of the weight and glory of the true cross.

The contemporary cross empowers the sinner. It is more a matter of Jesus dying to make me into a bigger and better me—Jesus dying to help me fulfill *my* destiny. So somehow the Gospel of Jesus Christ evolved into the gospel of improved humanity. This new, disfigured Gospel starts with me and who I am. In this perspective, God exists to simply fulfill my life ambitions and empower me to be the best "me" I can be.

Self-help with some Jesus language mixed in is not the Gospel. The cross is not about improving your self; it is about crucifying the old man and living from your new identity—*in Christ*. But this superficial Gospel is part of the larger superficiality in the American Church today. Sometimes it can be expressed in megachurches, but sometimes it is just as prevalent in small settings. It is a perspective we need to recognize and repent of so that we can move forward into the fullness of God's purposes on the earth.

THE HOPE OF REVIVAL

All this being said, in light of our present state, I am not pessimistic at all. I am very optimistic about the future! I am tremendously hopeful because of God and because of what He has put in my heart.

Naturally speaking, I would be very pessimistic. Naturally speaking, I would look at the state of this nation and the condition of the world and say that we have never gone this low before in so many different ways.

Looking at America in particular, I would say that—in the natural—there is no way back. Looking at the church, I would say there is too much compromise; there is too much worldliness; there is too much departure from the foundations of the faith.

But looking at God, I am full of faith and confidence because awakenings have come in our history during times when everything looked bleak and impossible. In his *Lectures on Revivals of Religion*, Charles Finney wrote that "a 'Revival of Religion' presupposes a declension."[1]

This is where we start, by recognizing our need. That is the solution to our present condition. Declension confronts us with our present condition and desperate need. Finney explains that religion is *not* merely some excited feeling. The problem is that in our carnal culture, we have become too excitable by the wrong things. True revival reignites us to burn for the good and holy rather than living under a lie and burning with lust for the immoral and unrighteous.

The road to revival begins where we start recognizing our spiritual bankruptcy. And it is out of our sense of desperate need for more of God's reality in our lives that transformation begins.

DARKNESS BEFORE THE DAWN

As I look at the present darkness that is encroaching upon our world, I am stirred to hope, not despair. Let's consider some similar seasons throughout history where darkness seemed to prevail.

James Edwin Orr, the foremost evangelical revival historian, pointed out that there was a great spiritual decline in America after the Revolutionary War. So by the late 1700s, church attendance was diminishing. By the late 1700s, the Christian witness on some college campuses that had been founded as Christian campuses had all but disappeared. There were so-called *Christian* campuses where you could not find a single professing believer among the few hundred students enrolled. But this changed dramatically with a wave of revivals that touched America in the early 1800s. Who knew such dramatic changes were about to come?

Orr points out that in the mid 1800s—right before the Prayer Revival that started in New York City in 1857 and swept across America before being brought to parts of Ireland and England in 1859—there was significant worldliness corrupting society. He writes of the rampant sin, the corruption of society, the violence, the sexual immorality, and even rising atheism and different satanic expressions of spirituality. You hear those reports and you say it sounds like the same thing all over again. Yet this was the context that brought about the Great Prayer Awakening. This move of

God's Spirit swept through the nation and had a profound impact both within the Church and upon the world.

Most likely, there were those who were overwhelmed by the signs of the times during the 1800s and longed to escape the corruption of society. Amazingly enough, on the other side of depravity was nation-shaking revival. In like manner, America today is perhaps more ripe for revival than it has ever been since; in many ways, it is in the worst condition we have ever seen.

Certainly, in my lifetime, this is the worst that I have ever seen things. There is very serious defection, even from fundamentals of the faith, with professing Evangelicals questioning the rightness of things as basic as homosexual practice. What were once firm, absolute standards for biblical morality have become topics for debate. Believers are now discussing questions such as, "Is it possible for God to bless two homosexuals in a committed sexual relationship?"[2]

To be clear, I am not at all questioning God's love for those involved in sinful practices. Sin is sin—from lying to pride, to adultery, to fornication, or to homosexual practice. We have all sinned and fallen short of God's standard of absolute holiness. But because of Jesus and the indwelling power of the Spirit, we have been called to live as those set apart. God's unconditional love is not being questioned; rather His standards for acceptable living are. This in and of itself creates a dangerous theology, littered with half-truths. We create a god in our image who not only loves us unconditionally, but unconditionally accepts all of our practices, values, and sinful expressions. I've never seen moral defection on this level.

There is a greater tendency toward embracing Universalism and questioning whether there is a future judgment of any kind. These are serious theological defections that we must combat. Sadly much of the Church is moving away from the life and power of the Spirit.

The very Spirit Who has been given to abide within us and equip us to live the Christian life has become controversial and debated. We are even afraid of His movement in our midst. We are at a very critical juncture.

But this is not the time to bury our heads in the sand, rather it is time to openly and painfully acknowledge our present condition. And based on the history of past revival, I see that the season we are living in is an hour ripe for great awakening. It is only during a time of famine that you become desperate for the rain to come.

That is the state that we are coming into now.

CALLED OUT...AND CALLED UP

Most certainly, it is not the time for us to be fleshly critics of the Church. Prophetic voices like A. W. Tozer and Leonard Ravenhill *called out* so they could *call up*. For example, Ravenhill didn't preach and write with the intention of focusing exclusively on the Church's faults. Hardly. With honest voice, he spoke in no uncertain terms about areas of compromise within the community of faith. His poignant words were always delivered with hope. He called out issues so that the people could repent and start living the *true* abundant life. Such words are salted with the hope of revival.

In that spirit, let me end this chapter with a few of Ravenhill's quotes to stir up your hope:

> The Church used to be a lifeboat rescuing the perishing.
> Now she is a cruise ship recruiting the promising.

Church is not about recruiting those with talent and appeal—it is about being a life-saving community that rescues the lost from perishing.

A true shepherd leads the way. He does not merely point the way.

There are many church leaders today who are content to simply "point the way" to living the Christian life through their sermons, teaching, media, and books. The problem? Many teach one lifestyle while living another. True pastors and leaders will faithfully walk out their talk.

If Jesus preached the same message ministers preach today, He would have never been crucified.

Jesus preached and lived as a citizen of another world, another Kingdom. This is what ultimately led to His crucifixion. He loved radically. He performed great signs, wonders, healings, and miracles. None can compare to Him in compassion, kindness, tenderness, and grace. Yet at the same time, His Gospel went forth like a sword. It offended the status quo, calling them to leave behind the comfortable and familiar.

This same Savior is calling us out of safe places and into the adventure of a life completely devoted to Him. Even though the Church may embrace a new expression of compromised Christianity, Jesus is inviting you to join His ranks. Remember, *revival is nothing short of returning to the radical faith of the New Testament.*

Are you willing to say yes? If so, you are setting yourself up for a life of personal revival.

NOTES

1. Charles Finney, *Lectures on Revival of Religion*, "What a Revival of Religion Is," http://www.gospeltruth.net/ 1868Lect_on_Rev_of_Rel/68revlec01.htm. Accessed Sept. 4, 2014.

2.   For more information on this specific subject, you can read *Can You Be Gay and Christian* by Dr. Michael Brown (Lake Mary: Frontline, 2014).

CHAPTER 5

WHAT KIND OF GOSPEL ARE WE PREACHING?

There is a kind of gospel being proclaimed today which conveniently accommodates itself to the spirit of the age, and makes no demand for godliness.
—DUNCAN CAMPBELL

In the last chapter, we briefly considered the present state of the Church. I want us to explore this further and examine why we have gone down this road. If we can identify some of the motivations for embracing this lukewarm, substandard version of the New Testament faith, perhaps we can start avoiding the traps that so relentlessly try to ensnare us into this superficial, and sometimes even counterfeit, spirituality.

THE GOSPEL AND GOD'S WRATH

The New Testament Gospel starts with God and tells us what we must do to please Him. The contemporary Gospel starts with us and tells us what God can do to please us. No wonder we are in such spiritual confusion and moral malaise.

When Paul wrote to the Romans, he wanted to be sure they understood the true Gospel, and after declaring the Gospel as the power of God for the salvation of everyone who believes (see Rom. 1:16), the first major subject he addressed was the wrath of God.

That's right. The wrath of God. Today we dare not even speak about it.

But Paul knew better, stating, "For the wrath of God is revealed from heaven against all ungodliness and unrighteousness of men, who by their unrighteousness suppress the truth" (Rom. 1:18). He continued writing about this same subject for fourteen verses.

What? He didn't start with a message about God's love? He didn't start with a sweet sermon about how the Lord wants each of us to be happy and fulfilled? He didn't go out of his way to make sure that his plain speech didn't offend his hearers or hurt their feelings?

It is true that he told the Roman believers they were loved by God (verse 7), and he certainly exalted Jesus right from the start (verses 3-4). But he hardly preached some sappy, sentimental, feel-good message. To the contrary, he proclaimed that God's wrath against sinners was clearly revealed, that human beings had no excuse, and that all of us—Jew and Gentile alike—were guilty in His sight and in desperate need of His mercy. In fact, these were the main themes of the first three chapters of the book.

Do we think we know better than Paul? Do we have a greater revelation of grace than he did? Do we understand the Gospel more than Paul understood it?

The Brownsville Revival is not remembered for its sermons about God promising a wonderful, happy life if you simply believed in Him, although without a doubt, every night, the love of God was clearly proclaimed and the gift of salvation was freely offered. But today, even when we preach on the love of God, if we neglect preaching about sin, the wrath of God, and humankind's need for a Savior, we are promoting imbalance. When we preach God's mercy without the reality of sin, one must ask the question: *Why must God be merciful?* Why do I need mercy from Him at all? If we preach a Savior without giving context for what we need saving from, our grasp of salvation is limited. It all comes together when we present the complete, full Gospel—nothing missing, nothing lacking.

I still remember how night after night during the revival, a Gospel of repentance was faithfully preached. It thundered through that church in Pensacola, not merely swaying the mind, but piercing the heart. The result? People were lined up outside the doors from early in the morning to attend night services. There was something about the message that not only attracted the Holy Spirit, but also drew the people. *It is deception for us to believe that in order to bring people to Christ, we need to water down the message and make it palatable.* I have seen just the opposite take place.

God's wrath is aimed at sin, but because of Jesus's redemptive work, there is no reason for any human being to live under the tyranny of sin or the threat of coming wrath. Justification in the sight of the holy, righteous God has been made available to all who receive the work of Christ by faith. *This is the Gospel.*

It presents sin as sin, and in doing so shows us just how glorious the Savior truly is. Revival is nothing short of a return to the authentic Gospel.

THE GOSPEL THAT DEMANDS EVERYTHING

After teaching on justification by faith (see Rom. 4-5), Paul moved to the subject of our victory over sin, making statements like the following:

> *We know that our old self was crucified with him in order that the body of sin might be brought to nothing, so that we would no longer be enslaved to sin. For one who has died has been set free from sin* (Romans 6:6-7).

> *So you also must consider yourselves dead to sin and alive to God in Christ Jesus. Let not sin therefore reign in your mortal body, to make you obey its passions* (Romans 6:11-12).)

> *But thanks be to God, that you who were once slaves of sin have become obedient from the heart to the standard of teaching to which you were committed, and, having been set free from sin, have become slaves of righteousness* (Romans 6:17-18).

Yes, we find true liberty by being "slaves of righteousness." (Note also that Paul described himself as a "slave" of Jesus the Messiah—using the identical Greek word—in Romans 1:1.)

In that same spirit, Paul wrote, "So then, brothers, we are debtors, not to the flesh, to live according to the flesh. For if you live according to the flesh you will die, but if by the Spirit you put to death the deeds of the body, you will live" (Rom. 8:12-13). We are spiritual debtors!

I could cite similar quotes from almost all of Paul's letters, not to mention those of Peter, Jacob (James), John, Judah (Jude), and Hebrews, all with the same message: *Because we have been saved by the Lord Jesus, we are no longer our own, and we do not have the right to live for ourselves.* Rather, we have a lifelong debt to Him, and it is our joyful privilege to fulfill that debt, since living for Him is the only way to experience real life, which is eternal life.

THE GOSPEL AS REVEALED IN THE NEW TESTAMENT

Of course, Paul would be the first to tell us of the glories of God's grace, of the peace and joy we experience in His presence, of the extraordinary nature of His love, of the power of the Spirit who lives in us, and of the sacred standing we have as His sons and daughters. Yes, yes, and yes! (Read Paul's words in Romans 5:1-11 or 8:14-39 to sample two wonderful passages just found in this letter.)

Paul started with God, not with man (after all, He is the Creator, and we are the creation), and he didn't water down the message to make it more palatable to rebellious sinners. He didn't mince words when it came to detailing the nature of our sins, describing lost people as being "filled with all manner of unrighteousness, evil, covetousness, malice. They are full of envy, murder, strife, deceit, malice. They are gossips, slanderers, haters of God, insolent, haughty, boastful, inventors of evil, disobedient to parents, foolish, faithless, heartless, ruthless" (Rom. 1:29-31). He didn't describe nonbelievers as morally challenged, dysfunctional, and disoriented, but rather as disobedient. And that's why we need a Savior—not someone who would look the other way and wink at our sins (which would not have done us any real good) but someone who would take our sin on His own shoulders, dying for us so that we might live. What a Savior!

THE GOSPEL AS BEING PREACHED AROUND THE GLOBE

There are many differences between the faith we have embraced as American Christianity and what is being preached on a global scale. For nearly thirty years, I've had the privilege of ministering outside the United States on probably one hundred and fifty different trips. I have been to places like India every year for more than twenty straight years. Even though I witness various struggles and problems, I also see tremendous advancement.

On the other hand, there are places that are not doing well. European Christianity is struggling in many ways. There are countries that have been infected by the American carnal prosperity message, and a Gospel of greed has been exported. This is negatively impacting many parts of Africa.

> If we want to experience the power of the Gospel in our lives and churches today, we would do well to embrace the same Gospel the early believers did.

Yet in the midst of it all, there is a mighty outpouring of the Holy Spirit taking place around the world as opposed to the spiritual stagnation and backsliding we are seeing in many parts of America and the Western Church. While we are seeing a decline in church numbers, the global church is experiencing a massive increase.

There have been more people saved in the past twenty, thirty, or forty years around the world than at any other time in recorded church history. So God is moving. There are many people coming to faith in Jesus. And there are quality believers I have worked with around the world who have not been tainted by the love of this world and have not bowed down to the god of materialism. For them, serving Jesus *truly* is a life and death matter.

To give one example, the ministry we work with in India is led by a former untouchable. Early in his life, he responded aggressively to the treatment he received as an untouchable and became a violent Communist. He was an alcoholic atheist when Jesus appeared to him in his early twenties. Because of how Jesus transformed his life, his ministry has gone on to plant at least six thousand churches in tribal regions. The workers know that it could cost them their lives to preach the Gospel. As he baptizes people, he asks them, "Are you willing to follow Jesus to your last breath, to your last drop of blood?" That is the level of their commitment to the Lord, which is deeply and profoundly inspiring.

I am seeing very deep commitment around the world that is more difficult to come by in America: a radical devotion to Jesus that could very likely cost someone his or her life. This is exactly how the New Testament church community lived. If we want to experience the power of the Gospel in our lives and churches today, we would do well to embrace the *same* Gospel the early believers did. A cheap, glossy counterfeit simply will not do.

Isn't it high time that we get back to a New Testament Gospel message—the real Gospel—rather than the contemporary, watered-down version, which not only dishonors God but also does a disservice to people, ultimately hurting those we want to help?

Isn't it time?

CHAPTER 6

WHERE IS THE FIRE?

We are suffering today from a species of Christianity
as dry as dust, as cold as ice, as pale as a corpse,
and as dead as King Tut. We are suffering not from
a lack of correct heads but of consumed hearts.
—Vance Havner

There is a sad phenomenon in the Church today: bored believers! God's children are finding the Gospel stale, and going to church doesn't provide much relief. For some, church attendance at best offers a quick and temporary lift; at worst the weekly service is something to be endured. And outside the church buildings it isn't much better.

Revival is a divine confrontation. Heaven extends us an option— continue as normal or *recapture God's definition of normal*. I'm thrilled to see pockets and communities of pioneers in the Church today. These individuals have given their lives to further the cause of Christ. Normal *as is* does not satisfy them. They are going with the second option. They have caught a glimpse of what *true* normal looks like, as defined by the New Testament, and are pressing in with every fiber of their being to see that demonstration of faith restored in our day.

This is where the cry for revival comes from: holy discontentment. Our eyes see the gulf that exists between what was normative in the New Testament and what has become acceptable today. *Where is the fire?* The fire starts to burn again when we recognize that spiritual boredom is not our inheritance in Christ.

WHY THE BORED BELIEVERS?

In many circles, so little is happening. It would be bad enough if believers were discouraged, oppressed, or worn out. But believers being bored? How can this be?

The disciples in the Book of Acts turned their world upside down. When they were beaten and whipped, they rejoiced and sang hymns. When they were martyred, their faces glowed; even their greatest persecutor was gloriously transformed.

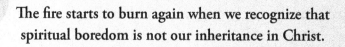

The fire starts to burn again when we recognize that spiritual boredom is not our inheritance in Christ.

Angels opened prison doors and earthquakes rattled jail foundations. Countless thousands were saved and multitudes miraculously healed. These believers may not have been perfect, but they were alive and on the move: day after day, in the temple courts and from house to house, they never stopped teaching and proclaiming the good news that Jesus is the Messiah (see Acts 5:42).

This was the early Church! Could there be anything more exciting? Even what Old Testament Israel experienced—including Mount Sinai and all the wonders—is almost nothing compared to a genuine New Testament walk with the Lord.

> *For what was glorious has no glory now in comparison with the surpassing glory. And if what was fading away came with glory, how much greater glory is the glory of that which lasts!* (2 Corinthians 3:10-11 NIV)

We are the ones "who with unveiled faces all reflect the Lord's glory, [and] are being transformed into His likeness with ever-increasing glory" (2 Cor. 3:18 NIV).

We are the ones God has lavished His grace upon, raising us up with Jesus and seating us with Him in the heavenly realms (see Eph. 1:7-8, 2:4-7). We are the ones called to be "blameless and innocent children of God without blemish in the midst of a crooked and twisted generation, among whom [we] shine like lights in the world, holding fast to out the word of life" (Phil. 2:15-16).

When Peter wrote about the reality of our redemption, he was almost overwhelmed:

> *Praise be to the God and Father of our Lord Jesus Christ! In his great mercy he has given us new birth into a living hope through the resurrection of Jesus Christ from the dead, and into an inheritance that can never perish, spoil or fade. This inheritance is kept in heaven for you* (1 Peter 1:3-4 NIV).
>
> *You are a chosen people, a royal priesthood, a holy nation, God's special possession, that you may declare the praises*

of him who called you out of darkness into his wonderful light (1 Peter 2:9).

Even angels long to look into these things (1 Peter 1:12).

But do angels long to look into what we now experience? The thought is almost ludicrous when considered in light of our contemporary expressions of Christianity.

THE GULF BETWEEN ACCEPTABLE AND A REDEFINED NORMAL

Are we glowing brightly in the Lord? Do the unsaved see the light of our good deeds and praise our Father in Heaven? It doesn't take much consideration to come to a simple conclusion: What we are presently experiencing is not what the Word of God describes. It simply is not happening in most of our lives.

These are not words of condemnation. In fact, I pray that you receive these statements as invitations to call you higher. There is so much more available for you to experience as a follower of the Lord Jesus. However, for our experiences to line up with God's normal, we need to start by committing to *follow* Jesus. *Casual commitment produces casual Christianity.* This explains why we are not seeing a greater portion of the Church ablaze with the fire of revival.

Yes, God is moving and working in this land. Many congregations are growing; people are being saved; the gifts of the Spirit are being manifested; and prayers are being supernaturally answered. But all this is occurring on an incredibly limited basis, in terms of both quality and quantity. It would be an insult to Jesus to suggest that *this* is everything He died for, that *this* is the evidence of the outpouring of the Spirit, that *this* is even a fraction of what God intended. No!

There must be something radically more—something of a completely different order, something worthy of the Lord—or the Bible is not true.

A GENERATION OF SPIRITUAL SOJOURNERS

Many of us have been on a spiritual odyssey. We have gone from message to message, from church to church, from conference to conference, from teaching to teaching, each time with renewed hope and expectation, each time thinking, "This is it! This is the real thing." And each time we have been sadly disappointed. The new teaching only took us so far. The new experience only went so deep. It was—and is—a poor replica of the New Testament faith.

Why do so many believers hear so many sermons, read so many faith-building books, follow so many spiritual formulas, and make so many efforts to grow, yet never seem to change? Is this what life in the Spirit is all about?

Let's be totally honest with ourselves and, for one moment, forget about all the excuses we have heard. When you read the New Testament, what do you see? What would you be led to expect? If you sat down and read the Gospels and the Book of Acts, closed your Bible, and pictured what would have happened over those next few centuries, would you have thought that two thousand years later the world still would not be fully evangelized?

Would you have dreamed that twenty centuries would come and go without Jesus coming back? And if someone were to tell you that by the year 2000 there would be hundreds of millions of "Spirit-filled" believers across the globe, would you ever imagine that the world could be in its present condition? More than twenty-five years ago, my then eleven-year-old daughter said to me after reading the second chapter of Acts, "If we had the same power they had, the whole world would be saved in a matter of months!"

LESSONS LEARNED THROUGH OSWALD CHAMBERS

Oswald Chambers, the godly author of the devotional classic *My Utmost for His Highest*, found a way out of spiritual malaise. But his deliverance came through a crisis that began when he heard there was more to be experienced in the Lord. This is where it must start for us. The born-again, Spirit-filled life is supposed to be different!

Chambers had come to know the Lord as a boy and, in his own words, "enjoyed the presence of Jesus Christ wonderfully." Yet it was some years before he totally gave himself over to the Lord's service; he did not hear about the baptism of the Holy Spirit until he was a tutor of philosophy at Dunoon College.

After listening to F. B. Meyer speak on the Holy Spirit, he went to his room "and asked God simply and definitely for the baptism of the Holy Spirit, whatever that meant."

Chambers said:

> From that day on for four years, nothing but the overruling grace of God and the kindness of friends kept me out of an asylum. God used me during those years for the conversion of souls, but I had no conscious communion with Him. The Bible was the dullest, most uninteresting book in existence, and the sense of depravity, the vileness and bad-motivedness of my nature was terrific. I see now that God was taking me by the light of the Holy Spirit and His Word through every ramification of my being.

The last three months of those years things reached a climax. I was getting very desperate. I knew no one who had what I wanted. In fact, I did not know what I wanted. But I knew that if what I had was all the Christianity there was, the thing was a fraud.

This is the revelation we so desperately need, as it is compelling enough to launch us into an impassioned, lifelong pursuit of everything that has been made available to us in Christ.

> God's assignments reveal His will to bring transformation even to the most hopeless and seemingly impossible circumstances.

WE CANNOT AFFORD TO ESCAPE

When we are fueled, just as Chambers was, by hope that there is *more* than we are presently experiencing, we are compelled to go onward and forward. *Forward!* These are the marching orders of our commander in chief in this hour. To reject this mandate is to willfully yield the state of our world over to darkness. This I am not prepared to do.

My personal walk with God gives me great hope because He faithfully puts promises in front of me. He puts assignments and challenges in front of me. The very fact that He puts these in my path is *not* so I can become a prophet of doom and gloom. God's assignments reveal His will to bring transformation even to the most hopeless and seemingly impossible circumstances.

God is not calling me to go out, build a big cemetery, and bury all the dead because it is spiritually over, metaphorically speaking.

We have seen the consequences of what happens when the Church disengages from culture and embraces an eschatology of pessimism and hopelessness, just waiting to be removed from this world, resigned to cultural defeat. Instead, regardless of your eschatology and theology of the end times, let us agree around the fact that as long as the Church is present in the world, we are called to be a catalyst for transformation. An escapist attitude prevents us from being the force of love, service, and salvation that Jesus designated us to be.

Consider this. There was a counterculture revolution in the 1960s that swept through America. One author pointed out that if you fell asleep in 1960 and woke up in the year 2000, you would find that the divorce rate doubled, teen suicide tripled, reported violent crime quadrupled, prison population increased five times, children born out of wedlock increased six times, people living together out of wedlock increased seven times—a massive moral decline. What happened? What was the Church doing during the counterculture revolution?

I believe in many ways there was an abdication, a checking out. We adopted an escapist approach: "Look at how wicked it is, look at how bad it is, Jesus is coming any minute…we are out of here soon!" The Church removed its voice from society, thinking it was on its way out. In turn, those who had other cultural goals—gay activists, radical feminists, and others with cultural agendas—became the revolutionaries. Those preaching a very contrary message assumed the role intended for the body of Christ to fill.

As a result America has been revolutionized. Of course, this revolution has been for the negative and not for the positive. So if our mentality is, "Look at the effects of homosexual activism. Look at how perverse TV is now. Look at how debased the movies are. Look at how the Church has lost its reputation in America. Look at this and look at that…It must be the end and Jesus is coming soon," what attitude does that produce? It produces one of hopelessness. It may produce one of excitement about the return of the Lord, but it does not promote belief for any change in the here and now.

We are left to wonder *why we should even try*. Why vote? Why take a cultural stand? Why do anything, because it is all coming down anyway? If I knew for a fact that the hurricane that swept through and damaged my home was coming back tomorrow—ten times more powerful—and was going to completely demolish my home, I wouldn't bother repairing it again. I would just get out of there.

This is a terribly negative and destructive mentality. Not only do we disengage from society, but also we don't press in, individually, to experience more of God in our own lives. We assume that more is waiting for us in Heaven, rather than experiencing some of it now, living out a vibrant faith, and serving as dynamic representatives for the Lord in our world today.

It is one thing to eagerly look forward to the return of the Lord and to recognize that until He returns we will not have perfect holiness or an end of human suffering. Therefore we long for His return. On the other hand, it is terribly destructive to think that "we are out of here any minute, everything is coming down, and there is nothing that we can do." The devil would love for the Church to buy into such a perspective. In the past we have witnessed Christians saying, "This is it. We are the last generation. It is over!" And that was centuries ago.

WHO KNOWS?

Instead of digging graveyards, spiritually speaking, I believe God's call is to build hospitals with maternity wards because there are a lot of babies coming. In other words, what God keeps challenging me about is to believe Him for massive spiritual change, to believe Him for the impossible, to believe Him for a holy upheaval. He is the God of life, and I am convinced that spiritual birth on an unprecedented scale is on His agenda for this hour in history. This ignites a fire within me to believe that nation-shaking revival is possible.

I believe it's possible because I've seen God work so many times in my own life. I've seen Him bring personal revival to me. In addition, I've been in the midst of genuine revival and outpouring that has powerfully touched so many people in churches across America and other nations.

My hope for the future is anchored in the character of God. I am confident in the unchanging nature of who He is: "His mercies are new every morning" (see Lam. 3:23). My fire is ignited by the eternal promises of His words, which urge us to call out to God and turn to Him in repentance and faith, believing that He will move. Could it be that He is simply waiting for those who would cry out to Him in desperation and sincerity? Could corporate revival in the Church be waiting on the other side of a revival in our personal lives—in how we live out our faith today?

This possibility of revival should stir us to return to the Lord and follow the biblical guidelines that would position us for the Spirit's outpouring. In Joel 2:12-13, we are given a blueprint for turning back to the Lord:

> "Yet even now," declares the Lord,
> "return to me with all your heart,
> with fasting, with weeping, and with mourning;
> and rend your hearts and not your garments."
> Return to the Lord your God,

for he is gracious and merciful,
slow to anger, and abounding in steadfast love;
and he relents over disaster.

Verse 14 gives us a stirring glimpse of what is possible for those who return to the Lord, repent, and rend their hearts before Him.

Who knows whether he will not turn and relent, and leave a blessing behind him...

This process begins with a stirring, holy discontentment.

CHAPTER 7

HOLY DISCONTENTMENT

O that in me the sacred fire
Might now begin to glow,
Burn up the dross of base desire,
And make the mountains flow.
—Charles Wesley

What we are presently walking in is not all it is played up to be. It cannot possibly be the same brand of faith as that which shook the ancient world. If our God "is able to do immeasurably more than all we ask or imagine" (see Eph 3:20), why do we ask for so much according to His will and apparently receive so little? Why do the imaginations and dreams we had when we were first saved seem like immature fantasies now?

WHERE ARE THE GREATER WORKS?

We talk about doing the "greater works" of Jesus, but let's be real—ten of us doing the same works of the Lord would challenge all of America overnight. (I wonder if there are even five of us who could handle such an anointing—along with all the media exposure—without letting it go to our heads.)

Preachers, can you be candid enough to stand up at your healing services and say, "If what we are seeing is a true reflection of the Lord, then He must be fickle, arbitrary, and relatively powerless!"

Evangelists, are you willing to boldly proclaim at your "revival" meetings, "If what we are experiencing is the fullness of the Spirit, then we ought to quit right now and go home!"

Pastors, will you express clearly to your flocks, "If the quality of life we are manifesting in the Lord is the best there is, then our churches are in trouble!"

Believers, do you have the courage to get alone with God and say to Him honestly, "If what I have is all the Christianity there is, then the thing is a fraud!"

God would be pleased with us if we did this. He was the One who said through His servant Malachi, "Oh, that one of you would shut the temple doors, so that you would not light useless fires on My altar!" (Mal. 1:10 NIV). That's right, useless fires—and God was the One who said so! He would rather that we close down the show if we won't clean up our acts. Why continue with our rituals if the Lord does not approve?

THE THIEF OF REVIVAL

Once more, these words are not purposed to bring condemnation. You, me—the entire Church—we all need to be called up higher. In fact, *higher* is that spiritual normal we are trying to get back to. The enemy of higher is mediocre. When it comes to the Gospel, mediocrity is often embraced when we mistakenly believe there is no place higher to go in God. This thought process in and of itself is a great deception that robs us of our cry for revival. Landscape-changing revival is birthed by a cry that sees *higher* and longs to bring one's spiritual experience into alignment with the possibilities seen in the New Testament.

The question is: Why are we satisfied with *useless fires* when the real, authentic, genuine, burning fire of God has been made readily available? Once again, I encourage you to let these words build up your spiritual tenacity, whether you are in full-time ministry or are a dissatisfied believer. We should embrace the following perspective: If I believe that where I am in my relationship with God is the be all and end all of my Christian experience, then there is something fraudulent about the faith I am professing.

Wouldn't it be glorious if ministers across the country said to their flocks on Sunday, "We're not having church today! We're not going on with an empty routine! No new programs or plans! We're going to confess our sins to God and acknowledge our spiritual bankruptcy. And we're going to stay here all morning and pray for revival."

What would happen to our country if congregations did this just one Sunday each month, without giving up or losing heart? The face of our nation would change.

WE MUST BECOME DESPERATE

We need to think of those we've preached to for years—with little sign of lasting victory in their lives—and cry out, "Where is the power of the Gospel?"

We need to remember all those who died of terrible sickness and disease—never receiving their expected healing—and cry out, "Where is the power of the Gospel?"

We need to walk the streets of our corrupt cities, looking at the addicts and alcoholics and prostitutes—in spite of churches on almost every street—and cry out, "Where is the power of the Gospel?"

We need to consider how the Mormons, Muslims,, and other groups are aggressively infiltrating our communities—while our own feeble witnessing efforts lack convicting authority—and cry out, "Where is the power of the Gospel?"

**We don't need more methods and techniques.
No! We need the Lord Himself to come down
and lift us up. Nothing else will do.**

We must force a crisis in our lives. More of the same will only produce more of the same.

Something fundamental, something basic, must change. Just building ourselves up with more faith, more consecration, more soul winning, more Scripture meditation, or more love will not turn the tide. All of these things are good. They are necessary ingredients to our spiritual lives. But in and of themselves they cannot deliver us from our present rut unless we couple them with deep spiritual hunger.

Our whole orientation to spiritual things must be altered, and altered from the roots. We don't need more methods and techniques. No! We need the Lord Himself to come down and lift us up. Nothing else will do. And when we seek Him with all our heart and all our soul, when our very being aches with desire for His visitation, when we are consumed with hunger for His reality, when we radically cut back on other activities in order to seek His face, then we are ripe for transformation. Then the breakthrough will come. We can be immersed into the very nature and authority of the Lord.

How miserable it is that "the average Christian is so cold and so contented with his wretched condition that there is no vacuum of desire into which the blessed Spirit can rush in satisfying fullness."[1]

THE ROAD TO REVIVAL

What can we do to position ourselves to experience revival?

First, we need to *recognize our need*. We need to confront both our personal need and our spiritual need. Jesus rebukes the Laodicean church in Revelation 3:17, saying, "For you say, I am rich, I have prospered, and I need nothing, not realizing that you are wretched, pitiable, poor, blind, and naked."

This process might be uncomfortable but it is ultimately life-giving. We can never posture our hearts for revival if we refuse to acknowledge the dead areas in our personal lives and walk with the Lord.

Second, we need to *understand what God has done in the past*: "I remember the days of old; I meditate on all that you have done; I ponder the work of your hands" (Ps. 143:5).

We need to read about revival in scripture, study historic outpourings, familiarize ourselves with the past moves of God, and connect ourselves with what God is doing in other parts of the world. We should listen and watch—do whatever we can to expose ourselves to what God has done and is doing. By studying the testimony of God's mighty acts, these stories stir hunger in our hearts and create fresh faith. The God who moved *then* can surely *move again*. The God who is mightily at work in a different part of the world is the same God in our country and nation!

Even though the idea of positioning ourselves for the next great awakening may seem like a giant mountain to climb, we must start to take simple steps in the right direction. God is looking for those who will make the consistent, daily choices to obey Him, to follow His Word, to study His works, and to live transparently before Him.

I went through a personal spiritual crisis back in 1982. God began to convict me as people were praying for me. The Lord showed me that I had left my first love. At first this seemed strange. I was an active believer. I was a serious believer. I was committed in many ways, but I had greatly neglected personal prayer and devotion. My personal fire for the Lord was flickering out. I had greatly neglected just feasting on the Word as opposed to studying the original languages. God began to convict me for leaving my first love, just as the church in Ephesus had (see Rev. 2:4). In the midst of this season, I started to recognize the distance I created between the Lord and me. I saw how far I had wandered from where I once was.

Even though I was still a committed believer, I was just a shell of who I used to be spiritually. I thought to myself, "I can fast and pray and I will be ablaze for a few days but then I'll quickly go back to the way I was." That was not going to work. I was up and down. I was inconsistent in my passion for the Messiah. Finally I said, "Here is what I can do. I can take a step in the right direction and take another step and take another step."

If you feel the same way, I want to encourage you to believe in the power of *one step*. You may feel as though you have wandered millions of miles away from God and from where you used to be. You might feel as though spanning the chasm you created between you and the Lord is hopeless—that God is finished with you. This is a lie. One step on your end is all it takes to invite God in. You might have gone ten million miles from where you were. Just take *one step* in faith toward God and be confident that He has made the ten-million-mile journey that you could *never* make. Then take the next step and the next step, and before you know it, dramatic change will come in your life.

DISCONTENTMENT: YOUR KEY TO REVIVAL

As discussed in the previous section, Oswald Chambers was not content with where he was, as his vacuum of desire was too great. He came to the critical juncture that the Holy Spirit is beckoning you to:

> Those of you who know the experience (of the baptism of the Spirit), know very well how God brings one to the point of utter despair, and I got to the place where I did not care whether everyone knew how bad I was. I cared for nothing on earth, saving to get out of my present condition.
>
> At the end of a little meeting, after singing "Touch Me Again Lord," Chambers said: "I felt nothing, but I knew emphatically my time had come, and I rose to my feet. I had no vision of God, only a sheer, dogged determination to take God at His Word and to prove this thing for myself. And I stood up and said so. That was bad enough, but what followed was ten times worse. After I sat down, the speaker, who knew me well, said, 'That is very good of our brother. He has spoken like that as an example to the rest of you.'

Up I got again and said, "I got up for no one's sake. I got up for my own sake. Either Christianity is a downright fraud, or I have not got hold of the right end of the stick." And then, and there, I claimed the gift of the Holy Spirit in dogged committal on Luke 11:13. I had no vision of Heaven or of angels. I had nothing. I was as dry and empty as ever, no power or realization of God, no witness of the Holy Spirit.[2]

But something supernatural *had* taken place. God had taken hold of his life. Four years later Chambers commented:

If the previous years had been Hell on earth, these four years have truly been Heaven on earth. Glory be to God, the last aching abyss of the human heart is filled to overflowing with the love of God. Love is the beginning, love is the middle, and love is the end. After He comes in, all you see is "Jesus only, Jesus ever."[3]

Looking back, Oswald Chambers could say, "The baptism of the Holy Ghost does not make you think of time or eternity; it is one amazing, glorious now… It is no wonder that I talk so much about an altered disposition: God altered mine; I was there when He did it, and I have been there ever since."[4]

STIRRINGS OF SPIRITUAL OUTPOURING

Just as the Holy Spirit stirred Chambers's heart to experience personal revival, the Lord continues to perform such a work even today. The signs are all there!

I would like to take you back for a moment to the season just prior to the Brownsville Revival. For some years, I had been desperate for divine visitation and outpouring. I was absolutely convinced that revival was America's only hope. Motivated by this conviction, I had been preaching and writing about these themes for several years, beginning with my 1989 book *End of the American Gospel Enterprise*, 1990's *How Saved Are We?*, and then 1991's *Whatever Happened to the Power of God?*

In March of 1995, I released the book *A Time for Holy Fire*. It concluded with the words "Are you ready?" I was convinced that something powerful was just waiting at the door. Revival was near! There was a stirring and the beginnings of a new outpouring, and I sensed it was right at the door, ready to break.

> **God is the One who alone initiates spiritual hunger; it is up to us to respond to it.**

I don't see that same stirring today, but I see an inkling of it. I see the beginnings of it. I hear more and more people saying that we've got to have revival; we've got to seek God. More and more major Christian voices are speaking again about our desperate need for a great awakening. In my view, this was happening much more in the late 1980s and into the early '90s than it is now. But I see it rising again. That is an encouragement. I see that sense of desperation and urgency gripping the body of Christ once more.

With Brownsville specifically, I was not at the church prior to Revival. But I know Pastor John Kilpatrick reached a point of absolute desperation during which he would shut himself in the church building at night and pray for hours in the dark. He would cry out, "God, if you don't come and visit, I can't go on." Pastor Kilpatrick will share more about his personal journey to revival later in the book. That was the kind of hunger stirring in my heart. That was the hunger that was in evangelist Steve Hill's heart. Among all of us, that combined hunger and thirst was something very powerful. God is the One who alone initiates spiritual hunger; it is up to us to respond to it. He stirs our hearts to hunger, and as we respond He graciously comes to fill the hungry.

I don't see us at that desperate point right now, but I see us getting there, little by little. That's positive. The question is, are *you* willing to respond to His stirrings?

Are you willing to become consumed to the core of your being with desire for God?

Are you willing to let Him strip you of all confidence in the flesh until you get to the point of total dependence on Him?

Are you willing—in brokenness and humility—to stand out from the crowd that is apparently satisfied with leftover bread?

Are you willing to be emptied and emptied again so that God can fully fill you? The choice is entirely yours.

How far are you willing to go?

In the next section, you will read the firsthand account of a man who became deeply discontented with status quo Christianity. Hunger drove him to a place of absolute desperation. Holy discontentment caused him to take action, and as a result he participated in and pastored a historic move of the Holy Spirit in his life, in his church, and, ultimately, throughout the world.

You will read the testimony of Pastor John Kilpatrick, who served as senior pastor of Brownsville Assembly of God during the Brownsville Revival (1995–2000).

NOTES

1. A. W. Tozer, *Born After Midnight* (Camp Hill, PA: Christian Publications, 1959), 22.

2. The account of Oswald Chambers's spiritual breakthrough is taken from Edwin F. Harvey and Lillian Harvey, *They Knew Their God*, vol. 3 (Hampton, TN: Harvey and Tait, 1988), 9-96.

3. Ibid.

4. Ibid.

PART TWO

OUR DESPERATE CRY

PASTOR JOHN KILPATRICK

I knew there was more of God to experience. This is what birthed a desperate cry in my heart. Even though I had everything one might consider as success—a growing church, a thriving TV ministry, a loving family—I was not satisfied.

As a boy, I tasted things of God that ruined me for any kind of Christianity that was less than supernatural. I experienced prayer meetings where the presence of God was so strong, so thick, and so tangible that grown men laid prostrate on the ground, unable to stand on their own volition.

THE FIRE THAT NEVER SLEEPS

This is not simply the faith that I was exposed to as a young man; it is the faith that Jesus introduced and the disciples demonstrated. Revival is the solution to our ills, in both the Church and society as a whole. However, revival cannot be optional. It cannot be one prayer request among many. Revival must become our desperate cry if we are going to see God move among us in authentic, New Testament power.

> *At God's counter there are no "sale days," for the price of revival is ever the same—travail.*
> —LEONARD RAVENHILL

> *You must pray with all your might. That does not mean saying your prayers, or sitting gazing about in church or chapel with eyes wide open while someone else says them for you. It means fervent, effectual, untiring wrestling with God.*
> —WILLIAM BOOTH

> *It is not enough for the believer to begin to pray, nor to pray correctly; nor is it enough to continue for a time to pray. We must patiently, believingly continue in prayer until we obtain an answer. Further, we have not only to continue in prayer until the end, but we have also to believe that God does hear us and will answer our prayers. Most frequently we fail in not continuing in prayer until the blessing is obtained, and in not expecting the blessing.*
> —GEORGE MULLER

CHAPTER 8

DESPERATE FOR ENCOUNTER

As long as we are content to live
without revival, we will.
—LEONARD RAVENHILL

I am convinced, now more than ever, that revival is the only hope for our nation. It's really revival or else. Our survival as a society is dependent on a revived Church. After all, as the Church goes, so goes the world. We need to seize the moment we have been given. In these days of deep darkness and moral compromise, the body of Christ cannot afford to remain a sleeping giant. While society as a whole, and even pockets of Christianity, are embracing sin as acceptable, the Church is abandoning the power of Pentecost. The very dynamic that set us apart to begin with is what many have considered unpopular, controversial, and divisive. It's time for us to go after revival with full force. We are not asking God for something new and different; we are longing for a restoration of the old, ancient, and powerful.

God is the only One capable of breaking into a human heart and setting it ablaze with holy zeal.

When the Brownsville Revival hit, I was *not* the most qualified person to pastor such a move of the Holy Spirit. Yes, I attended Bible school, studied church history, and have read several books on the subject of revival. I have taught on revival, preached about revival, and have longed to witness a mighty outpouring of God's Spirit all my life. But what *really* qualifies someone to steward a historic move of the Holy Spirit?

It's certainly not about ability. It's not education. It's not articulation, or eloquence, or even how good a preacher you are. I have simply given my life and ministry to being a custodian of God's presence. That's it. Over the years the Lord has raised me up with this being my driving goal. More than pleasing people, I have endeavored to accommodate God's presence. After all, true, lasting transformation only takes place because of an encounter with the Holy Spirit. Our gimmicks, no matter how great or flashy, don't have what it takes. God is the only One capable of breaking into a human heart and setting it ablaze with holy zeal. He alone demolishes strongholds, cancels curses, overcomes impossibilities, breaks addictions, heals sick bodies, and delivers tormented souls.

For many years I prayed a prayer that is surely familiar to many pastors: "Lord, pour out Your Holy Spirit on our church." It's a common prayer, and yet the Lord answered it uncommonly. I still stand in awe that such a prayer was so powerfully answered in my lifetime—and before my very eyes during the Brownsville Revival.

The Brownsville Revival was not the result of preaching; it was God's sovereignty colliding with humankind's desperate cry in the place of prayer. In my personal experience, prayer was one of the key factors that paved the way for this extraordinary move of the Holy Spirit. In fact, prayer was a catalyst in pushing me out of my comfort zone and positioning me to be in sync with God's purposes for revival. It all began when I was just a young boy. It's amazing how your personal history—no matter how broken, unusual, or confusing—if often the very element that God uses to bring you into divine destiny.

MENTORSHIP IN PRAYER

I started pastoring in May 1970, and Brownsville Assembly of God was my fourth church. In fact, I ended up serving as Brownsville's pastor for twenty-two years. I am forever grateful for God's hand upon my life and the divine investments He made in me throughout those precious years.

To understand my qualifications to pastor revival, you have to know where I came from. I didn't come from a heritage of Gospel preachers or impassioned revivalists. My father did not raise me in the ways of God. In fact, I came from a very broken home. My father walked out on our family when I was just a boy, leaving my mother and me to fend for ourselves. I grew up without a natural father or spiritual father, for that matter. This is why the influence of Pastor Raymond C. (R. C.) Wetzel was so pivotal in my life and ministry.

This godly man took me under his wing when I was just a young boy. I cannot begin to exaggerate the investment this spiritual giant made in my life and how he helped stir my hunger for a visitation of God's presence. He understood the power of sowing into the next generation. Brother Wetzel became my mentor as well as my spiritual father. Since my real father left us when I was only twelve, this man of God took the place of my real father.

Revival is not birthed through preaching, but through prayer.

After I was called to preach at age fourteen, Brother Wetzel came to my mother and asked, "Would you let me take your son and teach him how to *pray?*" I remember standing there and thinking to myself, "Man, I'm not called to pray—I'm called to preach!" But it would appear he knew something I didn't. Revival is not birthed through preaching, but through prayer. Our preaching is only as effective as our prayer lives. There are many fantastic orators and communicators, but just because someone can speak with outstanding eloquence does not mean the message will come forth with anointing. Brother Wetzel was preparing me for what would come years into my future—teaching me the priority of prayer and experiencing the authentic presence of the Holy Spirit.

He knew that if I was ever going to be successful in ministry, I had to learn to pray. His definition of ministry success might be a bit different than some of what we have come up with today. For Brother Wetzel, prayer was always prioritized above program. He truly exemplified what a prayer warrior looked like. As a young boy, I saw him as a master of prayer. To this day I am deeply thankful that my personal mentor was a man who knew God unlike any other man I've ever known. I mean he *knew God*. He walked with Him. The dove truly lighted upon Brother Wetzel, as he lived to accommodate the

Holy Spirit with his life. I never knew anybody like him. He had a brilliant mind and yet was the most humble man I've ever met.

God used this dear man to come by my side during one of the most painful times of my life. When I was twelve, my father officially left our family. Between twelve and fourteen, when I came under Brother Wetzel's mentorship, I was very depressed. Even though I was not suicidal, I just didn't care if I lived or died. The house I lived in had been filled with turmoil and persecution. My father was abusive to my mother because she went to church and he wouldn't go. He was worldly and despised her spirituality. Since he wanted nothing to do with Christianity, he became abusive when my mother tried to take me to church.

My mother was always humble and yielding to him. At the same time, she was a woman of incredible spiritual conviction. She told my father, "I don't want to go to Hell, and I don't want my son to go to Hell." She would take me to church and endure the abuse. She endured a level of persecution for her faith—not just for herself, but also for her children. I am forever grateful for my mother's investment in our family's relationship with God.

After experiencing my father's abuse, ridicule, and, ultimately, abandonment, I was left completely numb. During those early stages of my spiritual mentorship, I was severely conflicted. Even though Brother Wetzel was a godsend, my teenage mind wondered what in the world I was doing with this old man. I'd think to myself, "I'm fourteen years old and here I am, spending every night with this old minister, learning how to pray." We would be out at night, getting a bite to eat, and as we drove by the ball fields with the kids playing sports—with all the parents cheering in the stands—I would start to feel very deprived. In those kids, I saw a life I didn't have and felt bad about it. Little did I know God was shaping me for the greater things that were to come.

It was during this season that I learned how to cry out to God in absolute desperation. This perseverance in prayer did not come instantly, though. It took time. It took training. When I first started praying with Brother Wetzel, I really didn't know how to interact. Because of my father's abuse, I didn't know how to be comfortable around men. I didn't know what it was like to be around somebody like him because my father was so abrasive and so violent. Brother Wetzel was the complete opposite.

Although he was so gracious toward me, I could not think about how this mentoring relationship would continue. Sometimes it was absolute misery. There were times when I seriously considered giving up and abandoning his discipleship training all together. And yet it was because of this man's uncommon relationship with God and his authority in prayer that I received a spiritual deposit that would exponentially push me toward revival. At the time I just didn't have a clear idea of how his relationship with God could transfer to me. In the days and years to come, however, things became very clear—especially as I started to witness, firsthand, answers to prayers and supernatural breakthroughs unlike anything I've ever seen. Even though you cannot "coast" on someone else's relationship with God, their position *in God* can compel you to such desperation that you press in to experience *what they are experiencing*, no matter what it costs. I found this to be true with Brother Wetzel.

THE SUPERNATURAL POWER OF PRAYER

I remind you that each of us has an individual relationship with the Lord. There is no question about this. We do not get saved simply because of a family member's relationship with God or because a spiritual leader is committed to training us. Brother Wetzel's mentorship could not save me; it could only disciple me. Church attendance and Christian education are inadequate to bring us into a vital relationship with God; it is our personal response to Jesus that determines how we progress in our Christian lives.

With this in mind, I want you to consider the blessing of mentorship. Even though you cannot be born again through someone else's relationship with Jesus, I believe that through mentorship and discipleship, you can *receive* from another person's intimacy with God. You are summoned to walk as they are walking. This is not God trying to make you or me into a duplicate of someone else. I know this much—Brother Wetzel walked in a dimension of God's presence and power that made me hungry. Even though some of those early days of training were difficult, I found that my desire for prayer grew exponentially as I spent time around my mentor.

In those early days of praying, we would constantly "pray the lights out" every night. We were there until it was time to close the doors and go home. Some nights there would be thirty men praying with us; most nights, however, it was just Brother Wetzel and me. We did not pray based on the amount of people who gathered with us; we prayed because we believed God heard our prayers. The number of people who joined us was irrelevant.

Many prayer meetings are cancelled today due to low numbers. People just aren't showing up. We assume that lack of attendance means lack of power or effectiveness. Trust me, it does not. I want to encourage you, keep praying! Yes, keep praying even if no one is attending except you. *Pastor,* I would encourage you to find some young people in your church community to take under your wing and raise them up to "pray the lights out." This doesn't always mean praying until midnight. It just means praying *until* there is breakthrough. In the old days, they called this "praying through."

> Church attendance and Christian education are inadequate to bring us into a vital relationship with God; it is our personal response to Jesus that determines how we progress in our Christian lives.

You have no idea what is going on beyond the scenes. As you pray, mighty things are taking place in the heavenly realms. *Believer*, even if it is just you, your spouse, your family, or a few friends gathering once a week in a home, continue to *pray*. You may not see immediate results with your natural eyes, but trust me, there is a great deal going on in the spirit realm.

I want you to be ready to be surprised in prayer. This is exactly what happened to me. Even though I was young in the art of prayer, my faith began to build. It was not long after we started praying that supernatural things started happening in those prayer meetings, and I was absolutely shocked.

The things I saw in those days marked me for the rest of my life. This must be why the Scriptures so often invite us to *remember*.

> *I will remember the deeds of the LORD; yes, I will remember your wonders of old* (Psalm 77:11).

> *Remember the wondrous works that He has done, his miracles, and the judgments he uttered* (Psalm 105:5).

I remember the days of old; I meditate on all that you have done; I ponder the work of your hands (Psalm 143:5).

Remembering the miraculous acts of God is essential to cultivating desperation for revival in your heart. You remember the supernatural things you have seen God do—miracles, healings, deliverances, etc.—and those encounters become personal benchmarks. They remind you of who God is and what He is capable of doing. If He performed the miraculous *then*, He can and will do it again. Perhaps it will not be an exact duplicate and maybe not performed in the same way. Nevertheless, the mighty acts of God serve as constant reminders that a casual, coasting faith will not suffice.

The following story serves as a key spiritual landmark for me, even to this very day.

MY ANGELIC VISITATION

By the time I was fifteen, I had been praying with Brother Wetzel for almost two years. During these unique prayer meetings, there was great division stirring inside and outside our church. This was starting to weigh heavily on our spirits. Things had been stolen. Someone was shot and wounded outside the church one week. We were tired, weary, and beaten down. We were desperate for a strengthening touch from the Lord.

> Remembering the miraculous acts of God is essential to cultivating desperation for revival in your heart.

It was around midnight. We were walking around the sanctuary, praying for our church, our families, and our friends. This was definitely one of those nights we needed to "pray through." Police officers showed up routinely at the church building to make sure each door was securely locked.

That night two angels broke into the church through those locked doors. This is a literal account of what I saw. This was not a vision of the mind or even an open vision. I saw the angels with my natural eyes. Both of the sanctuary doors were flung open—doors that had been bolted and locked. I can still hear the loud pop of the tin doorknob hitting the plaster walls. All seventeen of us looked up to see two powerful-looking angels walk through the entrance. One turned like a solider and went to the right side in the back of the sanctuary. He stood there solemnly, filling that area from the floor to the ceiling. Right after him, the other marched by, turned like a soldier, and went to the left side of the church. He, too, stood solemnly, his presence reaching from floor to ceiling.

So there I am, just fifteen years old, watching these mighty angels enter the church building. I was simply awestruck. To this very day—and at the time of writing this book, I am sixty-four—fifty years later, I can picture it as though it was just yesterday. That one encounter is forever etched into my mind. I remember how they looked: beautiful and tranquil. One moment my eyes were fixed on these angels, and the next, they caught glares from the headlights of the cars outside. The angels were just as real as the traffic passing by the church. They did not have wings, but they were adorned like warriors. They just stood there, filling the church from top to bottom.

I thought to myself, "Dear God, I shouldn't be here—I'm too young for this." I was shocked, overwhelmed, and awed. My mind raced. "I'm fifteen. I'll probably never see something like this again. I have got to remember everything my mind can capture from this experience." Even though we prayed nightly, we had never seen anything like this before, and I was not sure what to do. I glanced at the other men and boys. Their eyes stood wide open, thus confirming that they, too, were seeing what I was seeing. This was no vision; we were standing on holy ground.

When I looked back at the angels, I noticed no wings or shields or helmets. I simply saw different hues of blues, pinks, and golden brilliant colors forming an aura around them that was too bright to pierce. They stood radiantly for what seemed like the longest five minutes I have ever experienced. It was clear that they were standing guard over the church. Then, as if they got an order, they turned like soldiers, marched back to the middle aisle, and walked right out the door toward the passing cars.

We sat in silence, absolutely stunned. No one moved.

FACE TO FACE WITH THE AUTHENTIC

This story clearly illustrates the power of remembering. When I think about that experience, I am reminded of the quality of lifestyle that is available to all believers. Settling for anything less is compromise. Will it always look like angelic appearances or divine visitations? No. One thing I do know is that Christianity is nothing short of a supernatural life. When we drift away from the dynamic demonstration of our faith, we are in desperate need of revival. This is where our cry for revival is birthed. Those supernatural moments that cannot escape our memories stir us to press in for more.

Reflecting on my encounter, I remember that when the angels left, the building was absolutely saturated with the power of God. Brother Wetzel slowly stood and walked toward the back of the church to close the doors. Like little children fearing for their safety, each of us followed on his heels as he made his way to the doors. When we got back to the area where the angels had been

THE FIRE THAT NEVER SLEEPS

positioned, we all fell like dominos under the power of the Spirit. The residue of power in that area was so strong, we could not stand under its weight.

The atmosphere was electric with the presence of God. I didn't just fall down and then quickly get back up afterward; I went totally out and didn't open my eyes again until the sun came through the stained-glass windows on Monday morning. Amazingly, those doors were still open from those angels visiting us the night before.

> **Christianity is nothing short of a supernatural life. When we drift away from the dynamic demonstration of our faith, we are in desperate need of revival.**

That was my first supernatural experience. It made such a profound impression on me that it became a benchmark for the rest of my life—and the rest of my ministry. Because I saw and experienced the *genuine*, nothing else would ever satisfy me. The emphasis here is *not* angels; it is the supernatural realm that angels come from. The Church was never established to be an organization; it is a community of called-out ones, filled with the Spirit of God and empowered to do the works of Jesus on Earth.

Angels represent one dimension of what our normal spiritual experience should look like. Scripture tells us that angels are "ministering spirits (servants) sent out in the service [of God for the assistance] of those who are to inherit salvation" (Heb. 1:14 AMP). Scripture communicates that angelic assistance should be typical for those who have inherited salvation. Should it surprise us, then, when we have an encounter with one of these heavenly servants?

Perhaps not. Nevertheless, we *are* surprised because this realm has become so foreign to us as believers.

This is what intrigued me about my mentor's response to our angelic visitation. What was unusual and extraordinary for a fifteen-year-old boy was *not* unusual for him. He had such a deep relationship with God that the supernatural had become natural to him. He explained that he had had a similar experience in the past.

When the supernatural becomes the exception and everything we do to build our churches, disciple fellow believers, and bring in the lost can be easily accomplished through our own natural efforts, we are living beneath our spiritual inheritance. We must get back to the power of God. Testimonies like this remind you of the divine power available in God's realm. Perhaps you, too, have personal stories in which you experienced God's supernatural intervention in your life. Maybe it was an angelic encounter. Perhaps you received a miraculous healing or powerful deliverance. Every memory we have of experiencing God's power calls us to reconsider what normal should look like. My angelic experience was not given to me just to be a fond memory of what God did in *years past*. That single event created a thirst and hunger in my heart to press in for all of God that I could possibly experience.

I will never forget that from that moment onward, things shifted supernaturally in our church. Everything just exploded. In the very next service, the power of God broke out at little Riverview Assembly of God. As the pastor began to pray, just before the offering, the entire church fell under the Spirit's power. Thirty-eight people, many of whom had been coming to church for years, received the baptism of the Holy Spirit that day. God was showing me how encounters produce momentum. Divine encounters are significant for our personal spiritual journeys, but based on what we do with these stories and testimonies, we can actually watch the Spirit of God breathe on them afresh and multiply our corporate level of hunger, thirst, and desire for revival. When you remember what God has done in your life and share your stories of His mighty power, these testimonies create hunger in the people listening. They want to experience the same thing!

This encounter became my point of reference from that point forward. If I faced financial trouble, family trouble, or Hell on earth, this encounter was my guide. I knew that if God simply showed up, or if He sent any kind of angelic emissaries, no matter how bad the situation was, it was going to change. Their very presence had the power to break whatever yoke I was facing.

Every memory we have of experiencing God's power calls us to reconsider what normal should look like.

THE CRY FOR ENCOUNTER

I share the story of this life-changing encounter as a key reference point. In the next few chapters, I want to talk about how our desperate *cry* for revival is expressed. Specifically, I will show you how it played out in my life and preceded the Brownsville Revival. This is the cry that arises from the place of prayer. What motivates it? Our discontentment with the gulf existing between present experience and *available* experience. Remember, just because you are presently experiencing one expression of Christianity does *not mean* that it is all there is to your walk with God.

Do you feel as though you are sleepwalking through your Christian life? Friend, this is not God's desire for you. Jesus did not die so you could wander aimlessly and powerlessly through life, only to experience reprieve when you die and get to Heaven. If you are a child of God, you were born into something profoundly supernatural. As you taste those divine moments (I call them *encounters*) where Heaven and Earth powerfully collide, and you become profoundly aware of how real and close the unseen world is, discontentment is birthed in your heart. Celebrate the discontentment. If handled correctly, it will lead you on a journey that will change everything. It did for me. After all, it is a pure discontentment, for it beckons us into the place of prayer. The goal in prayer is to bridge two worlds: God's world and ours. We are not satisfied with the gulf between availability and experience. Your encounters with God remind you of what is available, and your prayers express your desperate cry to experience everything that is available .

This is my prayer for you as we continue on this journey together. May the testimonies about revival stir your hunger to cry out for everything that God has made available for you to experience!

CHAPTER 9

THE CRY FOR GOD'S GLORY

All revival begins, and continues,
in the prayer meeting.
—Henry Blackaby

I have learned that revival is definitely *not* church as usual. "Usual" represents what we have become accustomed to—our concept of normal Christianity. When revival comes, everything changes. Normal becomes radically redefined. This is exactly what we must be pressing in for in the place of prayer. Revival is not optional for the desperate person; it is the *only option.*

REVIVAL IS AN OVER-ANSWER TO PRAYER

I like to call revival an *over-*answer to prayer. We cry out for one thing, having some vague idea of what we think the answer should look like. Remember, revival is completely supernatural. God sends it, and anything sent from God's realm carries His DNA. Paul reminds us that we serve the One who "is able to do far more abundantly beyond all that we ask or think, according to the power that works within us" (Eph. 3:20 NASB).

What takes place during revival is, without a doubt, outside the parameters of normal Christianity, as defined by modern religious culture. It's not church as usual because the magnitude of God's presence is infinitely greater than it is during average, normal church. *Presence* is the key distinguishing factor of revival, which we will explore in greater detail later in this chapter. For now, it is important to recognize that revival is qualified because of how God's weighty, glorious presence crashes in on a place and a people. This is where we experience the over-answer to prayer. When God comes with His manifest presence, our experience is far beyond our greatest expectations.

> **Nothing about revival is birthed in common places.**
> **If we desire to see God move in extraordinary ways, we**
> **must be willing to do some extraordinary things.**

Even though revival is an over-answer to prayer, it is still an answer to *prayer*. In the years leading up to the Brownsville Revival, the Lord lead me to establish a house of prayer in our church. By August 1992, and throughout that September, I decided that instead of preaching at our Sunday night services, I would pray for anyone who wanted to receive the baptism of the Holy Spirit. That first night, over one hundred people came forward to receive the baptism, and many more came forward for specific prayer. This was my first major decision to do church *unusually*. I exchanged the typical Sunday night teaching time for prayer. The next Sunday night was equally as powerful. The momentum was growing and there was no way I could back down now. The Holy Spirit made it clear to me that prayer was a priority we were neglecting. Our services focused on everything else—worship, the offering, preaching—but prayer has been reduced to a little bit of altar time when we prayed with the people.

In order to accommodate revival, we need to be willing to move beyond the comfortable and familiar. The Holy Spirit wants to move in every single church community in the world. This is a fact. The reason He does not is because many of these communities are unwilling to host Him and cater to His preferences. My decision to integrate Sunday night prayer meetings into the culture at Brownsville was monumental in preparing us for revival. This was not a John Kilpatrick decision; it was a Holy Spirit directive. He told me, "If you will return to the God of your childhood—if you will make this a house of prayer—I will pour out my Spirit here." Without His instruction, I might have continued on, stuck in the same old rut, doing what we always did and seeing what we always saw.

The truth is, *there is no quick and easy way to revival*. We are not going to have true, lasting revival without prayer. This is why God placed me with Brother Wetzel all those years ago. He mentored me in the very thing that was catalytic to revival: *prayer*. Not casual prayer. Not convenient prayer. Not common prayer. Nothing about revival is birthed in common places. If we desire to see God move in extraordinary ways, we must be willing to do some extraordinary things. If you want to experience the over-answer of revival, you must be willing to dedicate yourself to the place of prayer. Not in a religious, ritualistic way.

The reason we are going on this journey together is to give you a vision for what prayer accomplishes. When someone tells us, "Pray because God says so" or "Pray because that is what you should do as a Christian," there is little motivation to do it. We need a clear vision of what prayer can produce in our lives, in our churches, in our families, in our cities, and, yes, even in our nations. When we see what's on the other side of prayer, it is no longer a burden or chore; it is our great and high privilege as believers. To think, the great God has extended an invitation for you and me to partner with Him *through prayer.*

I had no idea how prayer would position Brownsville to become a place of divine visitation. To this day, I remain humbled and awe-struck at God's choice to make our little community in Pensacola a place where the Holy Spirit touched the masses and multitudes were launched into global mission efforts. All I know is that prayer is an essential forerunner to revival; I learned this through experience.

REVIVAL IS WHEN THE GLORY COMES

One simple way to determine whether you are experiencing revival is by answering the question: Is God's glory there? Unfortunately the word *glory* has become lost in a sea of Christian jargon. As a result we really don't know what it means anymore. When we don't know what it means, we don't have a vision for it. And when we don't have a vision for God's glory saturating our homes, churches, and communities, we will not cry out for it with great desperation. Divine visitation is marked by the unmistakable presence of God's glory.

In order to clearly define *glory*, we need to make the important distinction between two seemingly related topics: anointing and glory.

THE ANOINTING

The anointing is the supernatural endowment of the Holy Spirit upon a person's life to do the works of the ministry. You could also see it as a divine authorization to operate in the grace and power of the Spirit in your life.

In Luke 4:18-19 (NKJV), we see Jesus introduce His public ministry with these words:

> *The Spirit of the Lord is upon Me,*
> *Because He has anointed Me*

And then to explain *what* He was anointed to *do*:

> *To preach the gospel to the poor;*
> *He has sent Me to heal the brokenhearted,*
> *To proclaim liberty to the captives*
> *And recovery of sight to the blind,*
> *To set at liberty those who are oppressed;*
> *To proclaim the acceptable year of the Lord.*

The anointing has been made available to every single Christian, since every true born-again person has received the Holy Spirit (see 1 Cor. 3:16, 6:19). Be that as it may, not every believer draws from this endless well of supernatural supply and power. It is readily available. The question is, are you accessing everything that is available?

If you have the Holy Spirit living inside you, you have been anointed to do the works of ministry. God's presence empowers you to do what you could not accomplish with your natural strength and ability. The anointing gives you supernatural wisdom and understanding. The anointing makes you conscious of the Spirit's presence with you and in you. The anointing gives preachers unction to preach, evangelists grace to proclaim the Gospel message, prophets the ability to prophesy, teachers the articulation to communicate truth, and pastors the compassion to shepherd. The anointing gives you business strategy, creative ideas, and decision-making clarity.

The anointing of the Holy Spirit is His supernatural presence within you to do what you could not do with your natural human ability. It really is Heaven's authorization upon you to do the works of Jesus *on earth*—in whatever sphere of influence you have been called to.

THE GLORY

The glory is *not* the anointing—the glory is the manifest presence of God. *This* is the over-answer to prayer that I described earlier in this chapter. Even though all Christians are filled with the Holy Spirit, there is another dimension of experiencing His presence. It is this unusual expression of God's manifest presence that sets revival apart from church as usual.

Even people who are not anointed can feel and experience the presence of God's glory. This is common during revival. In fact, I saw it firsthand at Brownsville as those who were far away from God ran toward the altar night after night. Why? Deep conviction of sin? Yes. But what brought about this conviction of sin? Outside those doors, people thought everything was okay. Sin was tolerable in their lives. Immorality was acceptable. Addiction was usual. They did not become convicted of sin just going through the motions of their everyday lives. Rather, they *did* experience deep conviction of sin in an environment saturated with the glory of God.

This does not have to take place in a building or a church. Revival history is full of examples where the glory of God refused to be contained by a building. The preaching of Methodist founder John Wesley and evangelist George Whitefield did not win converts because of high eloquence or stunning oration. Although these men were both anointed individuals, there was an unusual measure of glory in their preaching. They could truly echo the words of Paul, who wrote,

> *And I, when I came to you, brothers, did not come proclaiming to you the testimony of God with lofty speech or wisdom. For I decided to know nothing among you except Jesus Christ and him crucified. And I was with you in weakness and in fear and much trembling, and my speech and my message were not in plausible words of wisdom, but in demonstration of the Spirit and of power, so that your faith might not rest in the wisdom of men but in the power of God* (1 Corinthians 2:1-5).

Paul's preaching carried the manifest presence of God. In the same manner, Great Awakening revivalists like Wesley, Whitefield, Charles Finney, and Jonathan Edwards preached and God's glory was released.

The people exposed to such preaching did not simply make intellectual decisions to follow Jesus; many were so deeply touched that their physical bodies reacted in various ways to the glory of God that was present *upon* the preaching. It was said that people were encouraged *not* to listen to the evangelists while sitting up in trees, in fear that the weight of God's glory would knock them right out of the branches.

In the Old Testament, the Hebrew word for *glory* is *kabowd*. One of the first places this word is mentioned is Exodus 16:10 (KJV):

> *And it came to pass, as Aaron spake unto the whole congregation of the children of Israel, that they looked toward the wilderness, and, behold, the glory of the LORD appeared in the cloud.*

What the congregation of Israel saw was the manifest, visible presence of the Lord. It was not conceptual. It was not spiritual language used to describe a feeling, expression, or an act of thanksgiving toward God. When the glory came in the Old Testament, the atmosphere changed. The people stood awestruck, often in helpless wonder. Priests could not continue to minister under its weight.

The glory is that weighty presence of God that can blanket an entire gathering—or even a community. Read the powerful testimonies from the first Great Awakening in New England or the Welsh Revival of 1904, and you will see entire communities under that weighty canopy of God's manifest presence. This is what I long for, and it is what I have given my ministry to protecting.

As pastors and leaders, we are custodians of God's presence. It is all about doing everything to make the Holy Spirit comfortable in our midst. When all is said and done, there is only so much that we can offer people. Whether you are in the ministry or not, there is only so much you can give those who are hurting and hopeless. When we encounter God's glory, we are exposed to the great solution to humankind's state. Identity is found in the glory. Healing comes in the glory. True purpose and meaning are discovered in the glory. Humanity lives blind to these realities because of its sinful condition. What is the condition? The human race became infected with sin because of the exchange in the Garden of Eden.

We were uniquely fashioned to live in God's glory.

RESTORED TO THE GLORY

One of the most significant things about sin is that it broke humankind away from its original position—living in the glory. The glory is both God's standard and God's manifest presence.

Sometimes we read familiar Scripture passages like, "for all have sinned and fall short of the glory of God" (Rom. 3:23 NKJV), and maintain a limited perspective of their complete meaning. When Adam sinned, he fell short of God's holy standard, most certainly. But he also surrendered his adornment of glory.

David mentions this garment in Psalm 8:5 as he reflects upon God's interaction with humankind, His great creation: "Yet you have made him a little lower than the heavenly beings and crowned him with glory and honor."

The same Hebrew word that describes the weighty, visible, manifest presence of God—*kabowd*—is used in Psalm 8:5 to express the measure of glory that humankind enjoyed in the early days of creation. We were uniquely fashioned to live in God's glory. In Eden, Adam and Eve were naked. They were always naked, but when they sinned the glory lifted and they realized they were naked. In turn, they started reaching in their own ability—trying to cover up their shame. Humankind has been trying to cover its spiritual nakedness ever since Eden. The only solution is the blood of Jesus.

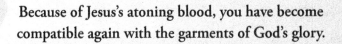

Because of Jesus's atoning blood, you have become compatible again with the garments of God's glory.

Spiritually contaminated by sin, Adam could no longer continue wearing a garment of glory. Sin made him incompatible with this state of perfection, and thus he fell short of living *clothed* in God's glory. In Romans 3:23, glory comes from the Greek word *doxa*, which refers to splendor, brightness, and kindly majesty. These words describe the presence of the King of Glory. Everything that describes who God is emanates from His being. His very nature *creates* a presence. In the same way that certain character traits seem to create an atmosphere around some people, be it good or bad, the same thing is true of God. We prefer to be around those whose personalities create a positive atmosphere of joy, peace, encouragement, and kindness. Consider what kind of atmosphere the nature of God creates around Him. Adam lived in this, but then fell beneath it because of sin.

This is why the Gospel is such good news on boundless levels. Because of Jesus's atoning blood, you have become compatible again with the garments of God's glory. This is why revival does not destroy people today. Even those who don't know God can taste a measure of His glory in the atmosphere of revival. In fact, the touch of God's glory is often what draws lost people to repentance and the prodigals to renewed devotion to Christ.

REVIVAL IS MARKED BY THE PRESENCE OF GOD'S GLORY

Revival happens when you can feel the weighty atmosphere of God's presence to the point that it becomes therapeutic. Duncan Campbell defined this measure of glory as a "community saturated with God."

Countless testimonies have been shared by those who experienced healing or deliverance simply by being *in* the glory of God's presence. No one laid hands on them. No one even prayed for them. God's glory just came upon these people and released such a therapeutic touch that if you were emotionally unstable or mentally tormented, it calmed you immediately. If you suffered a physical condition, that glorious presence would release healing. In revival, the presence of God's glory creates dynamic, measurable transformation in people. Perhaps one of the most common evidences of

God's glory in our midst is the frequency with which people are struck with conviction.

During church as usual, we may experience a limited measure of God's presence. It is only when revival permeates the atmosphere that there is an unprecedented outpouring of God's weighty glory. It is only as we experience this measure of God's presence that we discover what revival *truly is*.

I have traveled many places, and I cannot tell you how many times people have told me, "Brother Kilpatrick, I can't believe you are here! We're believing God for a revival." When you start looking beneath the surface, what these people are expecting and pursuing is not revival at all. They want crowds, recognition, fame, a presence on Christian TV, and media. For the heart sincerely desperate to encounter God's presence, revival is not an add-on to everything else we have embraced as Christian living. Revival is about rejecting the false and embracing the authentic. Revival draws a clear line in the sand. It gets messy and is often controversial. People are given the option to continue to embrace what the Holy Spirit is doing, on His terms, or go back to "normal." For the man or woman contending for revival, there is simply *no* normal to go back to.

This is when you know that a community is sincerely hungry for true revival. We don't pursue revival as an *addition* to what we are already doing as believers or leaders. Our quest for revival is motivated by a desire to exchange our ways for God's way. We pursue revival because we are tired of going through religious motions. A measure of success does not satisfy us. Popularity pales in comparison to enjoying the nearness of God's presence. A good job, a happy family, and a casual relationship with Jesus do not bring deep fulfillment.

What is the deep cry of the hungry and thirsty soul?

One thing have I asked of the Lord, that will I seek after: that I may dwell in the house of the Lord all the days of my life, to gaze upon the beauty of the Lord and to inquire in his temple (Psalm 27:4).

How lovely is your dwelling place, O Lord of hosts! My soul longs, yes, faints for the courts of the Lord; my heart and flesh sing for joy to the living God (Psalm 84:1-2).

As the deer longs for streams of water, so I long for you, O God. I thirst for God, the living God. When can I go and stand before him? (Psalm 42:1-2, NLT)

Our desperate cry is for God's glorious presence. *This* is the measuring stick of revival. We might conduct prolonged church services, hold meetings, and orchestrate events, but if there is no hunger for and encounter with the glory of God, we are continuing to do church as usual.

I don't know about you, but I'm tired of the usual.

CHAPTER 10

PRAYER THAT OPENS HEAVEN

*Every mighty move of the Spirit of God has
had its source in the prayer chamber.*
—E. M. BOUNDS

Revival is the supernatural result of God's people making consistent deposits of prayer. Even though there are other factors that contribute to revival, I believe one of the key catalysts is fervent, desperate prayer. Looking back at my childhood, I clearly see why the Lord schooled me in the art of prayer. Even as someone who felt called to ministry and preaching, it seemed odd that I was specifically mentored in prayer. Reflecting upon those years of deposit, it all makes sense. You can't teach people into revival. You can't preach people into revival. You can't program people into revival. The key to revival is and has always been *prayer.*

THE PLACE WHERE PRAYER WAS BIRTHED

In the previous chapter, I told you a little about where God brought me personally and where He brought our church community at Brownsville. He wanted to introduce some significant changes in how I approached ministry. Let me give you some context to the season in which we started Sunday night prayer meetings at church. Perhaps you will see glimpses of your own heart in my story.

During this season I was discontented with my spiritual life. By looking at the externals, I had no reason to be. We had recently built a new church building. I had a big church with a lot of people. I had the love and respect of the congregation. I had an international TV ministry with people watching from all across the globe. To many watching, I had it made when it came to ministry. But deep down, there was something missing. There was a longing in my heart for something more.

You can't teach people into revival. You can't preach people into revival. You can't program people into revival. The key to revival is and has always been *prayer*.

I clearly remember going into church one day and saying to the Lord, "God, I feel so guilty saying this. I've got everything to be thankful for. I have great children and a church that loves me, but I'm so lonely. And I'm hurting." I hated to say this to the Lord in light of every blessing I had to be grateful for. But it was just the Lord and me; no one was listening to our conversation. Because of this, I felt I could be painfully honest with Him. After I poured out my heart, the Lord began to show me that I had everything but a close relationship with Him. I wasn't seeing the fullness of what I was preaching. I preached one reality on Sunday mornings, but in my everyday life, I did not walk in this reality. I was hungry to experience the biblical truths I faithfully presented to our congregation on Sunday morning. I could not get away from this nagging emptiness within me. Thankfully, the Lord did not let me escape from it either.

One morning, as I sat on the swing on the back porch of my home, I had a confronting realization. This particular Sunday morning was very different. I could hardly get up out of my swing to go into my house and get ready for church. Truth be told, I didn't want to go to church—and I was the pastor! Out of concern, I asked, "Lord, what's wrong?" At this point, I began to earnestly seek God. Based on the state of my heart, I knew I was in trouble. That morning I didn't want to hear any kind of praise and worship. I didn't want to hear preaching, let alone be the one doing the preaching. I didn't want to preach one more sermon and not experience it personally. I was sick of it. So the Holy Spirit spoke to me, and He simply said, "Seek me." This is when He extended a powerful invitation to me: "Return to the God of your childhood—when you were under Pastor Wetzel." He said that if I returned to the God of my childhood, I would find Him. He was right. The God of my childhood was supernatural. The God of my childhood powerfully answered prayer. The God of my childhood sent angels to visit us as we prayed through the night. The God of my childhood was the God of the Bible, not merely a concept to be learned but a person to be experienced. *This* is what I became desperate for.

THE PRAYER JOURNEY

This ignited a fresh fervency in me to seek God in the place of prayer. I began waking up in the early hours of the morning, three or four o'clock. I'd get up, put on a pair of pants, drive around in the dark, let myself into the church breezeway, turn off the security system, and go in the dark sanctuary. Once inside, I would lie across the front pew and wail in prayer. There really weren't words that could express the cry welling up within me. I had no eloquence to offer. No one was watching. No one was listening in, judging my demeanor. In the stillness of those dark, predawn hours, I would walk the floors, grab my belly, and bellow like a cow. I would cry out in great desperation, "Oh, Lord, I need you!" Preaching didn't satisfy me. TV ministry did not fill this void. Having a big church with lots of people wasn't enough. In light of everything I had attained in ministry, I cried out with a deep groaning, "God, there's more. There has got to be more!"

Romans 8:26 truly came alive for me in this season, as Paul wrote: "Likewise the Spirit helps us in our weakness. For we do not know what to pray for as we ought, but the Spirit himself intercedes for us with groanings too deep for words."

> **The test of how people will steward revival
> *when* it comes is revealed in how faithfully
> they cry out for it *before it gets there*.**

I was tired of religious words and spiritual clichés. I was tired of preaching one thing but living beneath the very experience that I taught the congregation about. I wanted what was in the Bible and what was in my life to collide—to be the same thing. This is where the road to revival starts.

THE ROAD TO REVIVAL IS PAVED WITH PRAYER

As a church community, we prayed for two and a half years before the revival broke out at Brownsville. The Lord told me, "I'm going to do something very powerful in this house but you're going to have to make it a house of prayer before I do it." This is when we transitioned to our new Sunday night prayer meetings, trading the traditional teaching service for a time of crying out to God. In essence, the Holy Spirit was calling me to clear out the temple. When cleansing the temple, Jesus definitively stated, "My house shall be called a house of prayer, but you make it a den of robbers" (Matt. 21:13).

We are rearranging our priorities, both individually and corporately. If revival is really important to us, we will take certain actions to accommodate it—even before it comes. People claim to want revival. The test of how people will steward revival *when* it comes is revealed in how faithfully they cry out for it *before it gets there*. Our best preparation for revival takes place in prayer.

Prayer is *that* integral to revival. I will admit, when the Lord called me as the pastor and Brownsville as the congregation to make this new commitment to prayer, I was confused. Prayer meetings are typically the least attended functions of the whole week. The idea that the Lord wanted me to make prayer such a driving emphasis seemed counterintuitive to positioning the church for revival. How could it be that quite possibly the most unpopular activity in church culture could become a birthing center for a history-making move of the Holy Spirit? Even though it did not make sense at first, I had no choice but to follow the Lord's leading. I was so desperate that my ideas of how revival should come didn't matter anymore. I prized what *He* wanted above my own rationale and comfort.

This could explain why we are not currently seeing revival on the scale that Heaven desires to release it. Certainly, there are faithful bodies of believers across the earth who are giving themselves to the place and practice of prayer. There are entire ministries that are committed to night and day prayer. This resurgence of prayer is predictive of what the Holy Spirit is planning for this urgent hour. I saw this firsthand in how God was preparing us all for the outpouring in 1995.

In those years prior to revival, we needed clear strategy from the Lord in order to move forward with effectiveness. This is exactly what He gave us. Rest assured, if you feel directionless in your personal walk with God or your congregation when it comes to prayer, ask the Holy Spirit for divine strategy. He wants to make it practical and accessible. This is exactly what He did for our community as we sought to make prayer our great quest.

PRACTICAL BLUEPRINTS FOR POWERFUL PRAYER

God didn't just call us to pray and hope that maybe something would happen. He summoned us to the place of prayer and gave us a divine strategy to execute it. With this call to prayer, He gave us a promise: "I'll give you a plan, I'll show you the method." He followed through on His word, and I believe He will do the same for you. Posture your heart before Him. Recognize the importance of prayer in this hour. We can talk about revival all we want, but historically, landscape-changing revival has been preceded by tenacious men and women of prayer.

After introducing this call to prayer to the congregation, the Lord gave me the idea for prayer banners. We started praying around these prayer banners on Sunday nights. Here is how they worked: You would pray for five minutes around each of the twelve banners. Each banner represented a specific category we wanted to saturate in prayer. After someone finished praying for five minutes around one banner, he or she would move to the next one. By the time people had gone through the twelve banners, they would have prayed for a full hour. The prayer banners created movement and momentum for what God was doing at Brownsville. These nights of prayer became powerful launching pads for a congregational cry for revival.

As time progressed, we started praying for two hours. We did not start there, though. Some mistakenly assume that a prayer meeting needs to be spontaneous and unstructured in order to be Spirit-filled and dynamic. Spontaneity is usually birthed in structure. Without structure, there is no direction or vision for where you want to go. One of the problems we have all experienced with prayer meetings is feeling purposeless in our prayer efforts. If there is no system, order, or clear plan for a prayer meeting, it is easy for even the most "spiritual" people to pray for about ten minutes, and afterward feel bored. However, when you start with a plan, you have clear purpose in how to move forward.

Revival is birthed and sustained in the place of prayer.

So we started with a practical structure by using the prayer banners. As people moved from banner to banner, praying with purpose, their passion for prayer increased. What started as a one-hour prayer meeting soon turned into two hours. What began as a program shifted into a prophetic cry for the Spirit's outpouring in our community. Interestingly, the most popular prayer banner was the one designated for revival.

MAKING SUPERNATURAL DEPOSITS IN THE PLACE OF PRAYER

Without a doubt, these prayer meetings were catalysts for preparing the community for revival. They were like deposits in the bank that we could write checks from. Consider it for a moment. You can never have revival until you make the necessary deposits. Our two and a half years of prayers were the deposits for Brownsville. Your prayers are these deposits for revival in your home, church, community, and region.

As it is in the natural, so it is in the spiritual. You cannot write checks until you first make a deposit. You can never have revival until you make a deposit of prayer. Prayer is key, whether you are crying out for revival or are in the midst of it. When revival breaks out, you can't drop the prayer effort, because the revival will dry up. Prayer sparks and sustains revival. Once revival begins and you hit the well, you have to keep nurturing it. Revival is birthed and sustained in the place of prayer. Prayer not only opens the Heavens, but it also gives us supernatural insight into the ways and thoughts of Father God. He alone shows us how to sustain revival. We cannot live out a revival lifestyle apart from His grace, wisdom, and empowerment. Prayer keeps us under His divine influence.

When left to our own devices—regardless of how noble or religious they may seem—man is faithful to make a mess of revival. It is inevitable. We need to keep ourselves postured in prayer *before* revival and *during* revival.

Your place of prayer is your place of wisdom.

Natural human wisdom will not sustain or steward revival. It cannot, since revival is supernatural in origin. Only the supernatural can sustain the supernatural. Though we are fallible people, we have been given a place of access to the God who possesses all wisdom. Prayer is your place of access to God's divine wisdom.

Your place of prayer is your place of access.

We must remind ourselves that prayer is not just some tool to just *get* answers from God. Supplications and requests are simply one expression of prayer. In stewarding revival, we must remember that prayer is the vital exchange of communication between God and man, between the infinite and finite. Brownsville was not only born in the place of prayer; it was stewarded because of prayer.

RESTORING THE PLACE OF PRAYER IN THE MODERN CHURCH

I will never forget one Sunday night service as hundreds of people from our congregation prayed around the banners. They would pray forty-five minutes or so at one banner, and then migrate to another. As I watched this parade of prayer, I sensed the Holy Spirit say to me, "If they continue to make this house a house of prayer, I will visit it with My glory." I rejoiced. That was the word I had been waiting for.

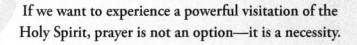

If we want to experience a powerful visitation of the Holy Spirit, prayer is not an option—it is a necessity.

I encourage you with that very same word—*continue* in prayer. Don't lose heart. Don't grow weary. Don't faint. Even if you see nothing happening in the natural, be assured that your prayers are a mighty force in the spirit realm.

When the Holy Spirit spoke this word to my heart, the story of Jesus visiting the temple flashed into my mind. I remembered reading that Christ had to *purify* the temple first. After he'd cleared away all the debris that was not supposed to be there, He could make it a house of *prayer* where people from all backgrounds and circumstances could come to pray. As the people began to pray, God turned His house into a house of *power* where He could heal the sick and deliver the troubled in heart. That power would then quite naturally draw praise and thanksgiving from the people, making it a house of *praise*. Upon reflection, these four steps—*purity, prayer, power,* and *praise*—are essential if we are going to see God's glory revealed in the Church today.

I am grateful for the believers across our nation and around the world who give themselves to the place of prayer. If we want to experience a powerful visitation of the Holy Spirit, prayer is not an option—it is a necessity. It is foundational. Whether one is truly desperate for revival is revealed in his or her response to the call to pray. It is demanding, yes, but the fruit that our persistent, continuous prayer yields is always an over-answer to what we *knew* to pray for. I knew to pray for revival. Based on the Lord's instructions, I knew to change up our Sunday night services and create the prayer banners. What I didn't know is where it would lead. What God sent us at Brownsville was infinitely above and beyond what my mind could comprehend.

One of the major hindrances that prevents prayer effort in our contemporary churches is an *easy believe-ism* approach to the Christian faith. We think that if God wants to do something, He will simply do it. If God wants to send revival, He will send it. This perspective is truly an abuse of the many things Jesus purchased for us. He has given us so much—namely, a voice before the throne of God. This is the place where our prayers and God's will collide.

Although the mechanics of how this transaction takes place are quite mysterious to me, I know from experience that revival is birthed in the persistent prayers of God's people.

For our corporate cries to get Heaven's response, we must honor the place of prayer once again. Jesus invited us to ask, and ask persistently, even though He also said "your Father knows what you need before you ask him" (Matt. 6:8). Asking reveals that God alone is our source of trust. It's easy to become self-reliant and independent when we believe we can do everything ourselves. When we ask for revival in the place of prayer, we are humbly acknowledging our complete dependency upon the Lord. He is the only One who can bring the transformation we are crying out for.

PART THREE

WHEN HEAVEN RESPONDS

DR. MICHAEL BROWN AND
PASTOR JOHN KILPATRICK

In this chapter, you will receive a special glimpse into the Brownsville Revival. This is a practical way of showing you what revival looks like and identifying some of the key factors that can release and sustain it.

Revival always involves an encounter with God's manifest presence. It is always supernatural; however, it does not always need to be spectacular in order to be supernatural. Your encounter with God may look different from what is described in this book. God touches people differently, depending on the person. One touch is not better than the next. The question is: How did you respond to God's touch? Whether your encounter was spectacular and electric, or subtle and deeply profound, personal revival is all about *your* response to God's unmistakable touch upon your life.

The purpose of studying past revivals, like Brownsville, is not to simply build a memorial to what God *did* years ago during a certain outpouring. Although Scripture encourages us to meditate upon the great works of the Lord, studying revival is intended to stir our faith to believe that a fresh wind of the Spirit will blow in our day. *Do it again, Lord!*

> *By the time the average Christian gets his*
> *temperature up to normal,*
> *everybody thinks he has a fever!*
> —WATCHMAN NEE

> *The Book of Acts of the Holy Spirit is a revelation*
> *of the way God the Holy Spirit, Who is fully God,*
> *wants to continue to act through the Church.*
> —F. F. BOSWORTH

CHAPTER 11

WHEN THE HEAVENS OPEN

PASTOR JOHN KILPATRICK

The average man is not going to be impressed by our publicity, our posters or our programs, but let there be a demonstration of the supernatural in the realm of religion, and at once man is arrested.
—DUNCAN CAMPBELL

A GLORIOUS FATHER'S DAY GIFT

It was on Father's Day, 1995, when our deposits of prayer started yielding a supernatural return. I will never forget the magnitude to which I experienced God's presence on that incredible day.

I hit the floor and was down for about four hours. Just to give you some context, I've been down on the floor, "slain in the Spirit" before but I have never encountered it like I did that Father's Day. What happened? The glory came and touched my human flesh. That *kabowd* weightiness of God's manifest presence collided with me. It felt as if I weighed ten thousand pounds. It was dramatic, but not scary. It was not smothering or anything like that. It just felt as if I weighed ten thousand pounds, and I literally could not get up off the ground.

I had preached on God's glory; now I was experiencing it. Truly, the Lord heard my cry. Truly, this was when God's glory became more than a Bible concept to me. I tasted it as a living reality. It's amazing how God will faithfully cause you to experience what you preach. That Father's Day was the great evidence of this in my life and ministry. I had taught about the glory. I was crying out for the glory. I could not continue to function as normal *without* the glory. What happened? God faithfully revealed Himself and encountered me in a way that profoundly changed my life forever.

As I lay there I tried to speak, but I could not even move my lips. That's how heavy the presence of God was in that place. Under my breath I managed to simply ask the Lord, "God, what is this?" The first thing the Holy Spirit said before He fully answered my question was "Happy Father's Day." What an incredible, full-circle moment in my life.

> I learned you can preach truth with great conviction, authority, and insight, but until you experience it for yourself, you don't know what you're talking about.

Growing up, my father was absent and abusive. My mother used to say, "Son, I feel so sorry for you because you don't have a daddy."

She passed away five weeks before revival broke out at Brownsville. As you can imagine, her passing was still heavy on my heart that day. She had always been there for me over the years. As a child, she would hug and kiss me, apologetically saying, "I'm so sorry for you because you don't have a daddy." I'd try to tell her, "It's okay. You're my momma *and* my daddy!" Perhaps never more than on June 18, 1995, did I become so keenly aware of God as my Father.

On the floor, the Lord touched my heart deeply when He said, "Happy Father's Day." It was like a confirming sign that He had poured out His Spirit on that particular day for a reason. He then said, "This is exactly what you got through preaching. *This* is my glory." I talked about God's glory; now He was showing me His glory. That day I learned you can preach truth with great conviction, authority, and insight, but until you experience it for yourself, you don't know what you're talking about. This is absolutely true when it comes to God's presence and glory. To preach it as a concept is limiting. To teach God's glory as a theological idea, not as active and available experience, is to shortchange the very truth of His presence. To fully know a person, closeness is essential. There is only so much you can receive through secondhand information. The same is true for God. Sadly, many are teaching secondhand information about a person we are called to know and experience. For example, a lot of people preach a theology of the baptism of the Holy Spirit, but unless you've experienced the Spirit's baptism for yourself, you cannot fully preach it. You have to *taste* and see that the Lord is good! (See Psalm 34:8.)

I encourage you to approach the Bible differently. Don't be content to live beneath what Jesus has made legally yours. Christianity is so much more than going to church, reading the Bible, attending a small group, and occasionally going on a mission trip. These are wonderful things, but trust me, I've had them all. I've had a big church. I've had the TV ministry. I have a wonderful family. I've experienced everything that should spell ministry success, and still I ached for more. It was this very cry that God so powerfully answered when He poured out His Spirit at Brownsville.

Let me give you some advice on reading Scripture: Let the Bible serve as your invitation to experience the God you are reading about. Let theology ignite your heart to encounter God based on what Scripture reveals about His attributes and character. Let the Book of Acts become your model for today, not just a memorial to what God did *back then*. I don't teach this as a concept. I cannot. I know revival is an available reality because I pressed in for it, and God overwhelmed my life with His glory. I believe He wants to do the same for you.

SUPERNATURAL OR SPECTACULAR?

You can experience God the same way I did on that Father's Day! Will your encounter look *exactly* like mine? Maybe not. You can't assume that the supernatural always has to be spectacular. Can it be? Absolutely. In fact, I would always keep your heart open to the possibility of the "spectacular" happening in your life. Don't be closed off to the idea of the Holy Spirit crashing in on your life or church like He did at Brownsville. In studying revival history, this much I know: The experiences are different, but the fruit is the same. From Charles Finney to D. L. Moody to William Seymour, the specifics of their God encounters were vastly different. Though the details varied, the impact was the same across the board.

Don't get caught up in specific feelings, manifestations, sensations, or physical reactions. When you know it's God touching you, regardless of what it looks or feels like, open your heart to what He is doing. His presence may come like fire, or His voice may speak as subtle as a whisper. One thing I've learned over the years is that an almost-silent whisper from God can produce more sustained, supernatural fruit than a fiery, dramatic experience. It is all about what *you* are willing to do with what *you* received. Sadly, people shrug off their encounters and become discouraged because their experiences with God didn't look like someone else's. The goal of this book is not to promote one unique style of God encounter. Rather, it is to show you how to sustain a practical lifestyle where you posture yourself as constantly available for the Lord to draw near and touch your life.

The Psalmist describes it this way, "Deep calls to deep at the roar of your waterfalls" (Ps. 42:7). Your heart will never be satisfied by anything or anyone in this world. It is utterly impossible. You will search, but always come up short. You will pursue, but live in continual disappointment. You will reach for the higher high and more exciting thrill, only to discover that your heart cries out, "More!" Don't let anyone tell you this cry is wrong or not of God; it most certainly is Heaven-born. The problem is that we are looking in all the wrong places for this pure desire to be satisfied. This is why encounters with God are so vital for us today. They remind us there is always more.

THE SOUNDS OF REVIVAL

When the day of Pentecost arrived, they were all together in one place. And suddenly there came from heaven a sound like a mighty rushing wind, and it filled the entire house where they were sitting (Acts 2:1-2).

As I lay on the floor that Father's Day morning at Brownsville, I could actually hear the Holy Spirit touching people. I couldn't see anything because I couldn't even open my eyes due to the weight of God's glory upon me. All I could was hear the Holy Spirit touching the congregation by the hundreds over in one section of the sanctuary. Words fail to articulate this experience. It was as if revival had a sound, and I heard it like a mighty wave, crashing from one end of the church to the other. I heard people up in the back balcony being touched by the hundreds. Then I heard the sound moving over to the other side of the church and touching people there. After a while, everybody had been touched and had had a unique encounter with God.

> **I know if I were to live to be five hundred years old, I will never forget the sound of revival.**

When all those voices merged together it was absolutely mind-blowing. I was overwhelmed on many levels. You see, if Brownsville had been a more emotionally expressive church, I would not have been so shocked and surprised. But it was not. Brownsville Assembly of God was a strong, high-integrity church. Our community consisted of hardworking people—a lot of government officials, Navy, and civil service people. These were everyday people who were upstanding citizens in the community, loved their pastor, and were committed to the church. We all had a rich history together, as I had been there for thirteen years before revival broke out. I knew everybody in that church by his or her first name. We were a solid, stable, Bible-based community. Perhaps this is why God considered Brownsville a fit resting place for His Spirit. It would be obvious that the cries of the people were *not* fleshly or the result of manipulation. Our people were not given to that kind of thing. In fact, I had a very low tolerance for fleshly emotionalism. Listening to those sounds and cries of revival reminded me how God has a tendency to use the unlikely to accomplish His purpose. We were an unlikely group to be touched by His power in such a demonstrative way—myself included!

When revival hit that morning and I was listening to the sound of voices uniting and crying out to God, I was struck. I said to the Lord, "God, please don't ever let me forget this sound." He has been faithful to that request. I know if I were to live to be five hundred years old, I will never forget the sound of revival. It sounded like a train rumbling through the church. You could feel the church vibrating. It was as though the heavens opened, the roof was blown off, and we entered into some kind of vortex. No doubt, Heaven invaded our sanctuary that day. That sound of God's power touching our community remains unforgettable. This memory remains a life-giving well of spiritual encounter that I draw from often. Just like my childhood experience of seeing the two angels enter the church is a memory that I draw life from, so is that moment when the sound of revival broke into our world on Father's Day, 1995.

Fast forward to July 2010. When British evangelist Nathan Morris came to our church in Alabama, I heard the sound come back. It happened at the end of a conference we hosted called Open the Heavens. The glory came in again and the Holy Spirit began a unique work among us. This revival (the Bay Revival) was different than Brownsville. Same glorious presence of God, same end results—different points of emphasis. Both were similar in that they focused on saving the lost and were highlighted by an outpouring of God's thick, weighty glory.

During the Bay Revival, however, there was a significant increase of God's miraculous activity. People were healed at Brownsville, but physical healing was never an emphasis—repentance was. At the Bay Revival, God's power flowed in an unusual way, bringing divine healing to many, many sick people.[1] Major miracles took place on a regular basis. Blind eyes and deaf ears popped open. Terminal diseases were reversed. Perhaps the most notable miracle happened to worship leader and pastor Delia Knox.

This godly woman had been paralyzed from the waist down and wheelchair-bound since Christmas Day, 1987, after a "drunk driver ploughed into her car."[2] She came to the Bay Revival not even looking for a miracle, but hungry to be in God's presence. The night when Delia came to the revival, she received a powerful touch from the Holy Spirit. She started to walk after having been paralyzed for twenty-three years… and she has been walking every since! What a worshipper she was and is. Incredibly, Delia's miracle story was featured in the UK newspaper *The Daily Mail*.[3]

> No matter what your moment in God's presence looks like, be it spectacular or subtle, it is altogether supernatural.

THE SONG OF REVIVAL

Just as prayer is a key to usher in revival, powerful praise and worship are necessary elements to sustain revival. At the Brownsville Revival, we were truly honored to have Lindell Cooley serving as worship leader/minister of music. Although he is an outstanding musician, Lindell is a minstrel and psalmist with a God-given ability to lead individuals into the presence of the Lord.

Each night during the revival, Lindell would take his place behind the keyboard and begin the worship. Some nights it would be a short period of time, and some nights it might take a little longer, but at some point during worship, he would get a certain look on his face; and that is when the glory would come into the room.

You could hear the sound in his voice; and when that sound came, it would always usher in the glory. Night after night, he faithfully led us into the throne room. There were times when the worship was so intense, that the accompanying voices of angels could be heard.

Lindell penned many songs during the revival, and his music went out to the nations. Many times as churches around the world would worship with his music, the same glory would come into the congregations.

He began his journey and his love for worship while attending camp revival meetings with his parents as a young boy. Through the years, the call of God on his life became evident. While looking for a worship leader before revival broke out at Brownsville, I felt very strongly that Lindell was the person that God was choosing to lead our church in worship. Without a doubt, I now know that no one could have fulfilled the responsibility of leading millions into an encounter with the Lord in the same way that Lindell did.

Even after revival services had concluded at Brownsville, and we all went our separate ways, anytime we would get back together, that same anointing was on Lindell. Why? He was and is a man committed to hosting God's presence. May this be our approach to worship in our church communities today. It's not about doing the latest, most popular songs or even following certain fads. Instead, worship is about accommodating the Holy Spirit's presence in our midst, both preparing an atmosphere for revival and sustaining the fires of outpouring once revival comes.

ONE TOUCH CHANGES EVERYTHING

When I read about how God transformed a region during the Welsh Revival, or how He invaded New England during the Great

Awakening with Jonathan Edwards, or how the Holy Spirit broke out at Azusa Street in 1906, or how His power saturated the community of Hebrides with Duncan Campbell, or how the people lined up outside Brownsville Assembly of God in the blazing heat of Pensacola to hear messages about sin, repentance, and the cross, my heart is gripped. All these accounts remind me that there is *more* to Christianity than I am presently experiencing.

When I read about the preaching of men like John Wesley, Jonathan Edwards, Charles Finney, or George Whitefield, the overwhelming message is that *there is more.* They did not deliver Christian life lessons; they spoke as oracles of the Lord. When they preached the word, the atmosphere shifted. People were so deeply gripped that they could not stand under the weight of God's presence and conviction.

No matter what your moment in God's presence looks like, be it spectacular or subtle, it is altogether supernatural. Always remember those moments when your humanity collides with His divine presence. It is in these experiences where you are reminded that God is real. He is not some religious myth. He is not a celestial clockmaker, who wound up the world and is letting it go on its own course. God is alive and desires to use *you* as His representative to show the world *just how real He truly is.*

The apostle John makes a profound statement by recognizing that "as he is so also are we in this world" (John 20:21 MSG). *As he is, so are we.* Jesus is alive, correct? Jesus is a real person, right? If these realities are true, then we must upgrade our Christian experience to agree with them. We are to live *as Jesus is.* This suggests that we are to walk this earth as representatives of the risen, living Christ. Revival is a catalyst that reintroduces us to these fundamental truths.

Before Jesus ascended back into Heaven, He gave the following assignment: "Just as the Father sent me, I send you" (Jn. 20:21, Message). Jesus was sent to earth to reveal and to restore. He was sent to reveal God to the people and to restore humanity's broken connection to the Father. This is your commission, as well.

God touches His people in the place of revival for a very clear purpose. It is not for some spiritual thrill. It is not to merely experience charismatic manifestations or emotional responses. The Spirit of God touches us so that we can become more empowered of transformation on the earth. His touch awakens, ignites, and revives us to be the Kingdom ambassadors Jesus redeemed us to be!

NOTES

1. You can view healing testimony videos from the Bay Revival meetings at http://bayrevival.org/media.php.

2. Daily Mail Reporter, "It's a Miracle! After 23 Years in a Wheelchair, Woman Walks Again and Says It Is All down to Spiritual Healing," *Daily Mail Online*, December 22, 2010, http://www.dailymail.co.uk/news/article-1340497/I -walked-walked-I-felt-like-I-entered-realm-Woman-paralysed -23-years-ago-cured-British-spiritual-healer.html.

3. Ibid.

CHAPTER 12

THE PRIZE OF GOD'S MANIFEST PRESENCE

DR. MICHAEL BROWN

You can have all of your doctrines right—
yet still not have the presence of God.
—LEONARD RAVENHILL

The presence of God in revival is everything.

As John Kilpatrick and I stood together at Steve Hill's memorial service, we began to worship. I leaned over and told Pastor Kilpatrick, "You know, a service that's three hours long is really, really boring unless the presence of God is there." God was faithful to visit us that night as we commemorated Steve's home-going.

This mighty general who God raised up to usher souls into the Kingdom recognized that without God's presence, there was no purpose. We might as well have gone home and ended the meeting. Steve did not rely on his oratory skills or intellect as he preached the Gospel night after night during the Brownsville Revival. He was simply a man who yearned for God's manifest presence more than anything. May the same be said of us today as we cry out for revival and visitation on our land.

> Revival is not a matter of us preaching harder, praying harder, singing harder, or trying harder. Revival is a matter of God coming in power and visitation.

EVERYTHING FLOWS OUT OF GOD'S PRESENCE

If revival is a season of unusual divine visitation, then everything flows out of the presence of God. Truly, revival is when God does what we cannot do. His presence among us should serve as constant notice that to sustain an environment, culture, and lifestyle of revival, we must be wholly dependent upon God. God and His presence are not two separate entities. His presence is not some mystical element. Even though the Holy Spirit indwells every Christian, we experience a unique visitation of God's manifest presence during seasons of revival.

Revival is not a matter of us preaching harder, praying harder, singing harder, or trying harder. Revival is a matter of God coming in power and visitation. Revival is not about humankind forcing God's hand to gain an objective; it is about flowing with the movement of His Spirit to experience Heaven's objective.

While there is an appropriate stewardship that we must assume while navigating through seasons of outpouring, it is vital that we keep our hands *off* the work of the Lord. The great prize of revival is this sense of God's presence, so close and so heavy among us. It is both glorious and tangible. No other element in the universe can so powerfully move people to joy, tears, laughter, shouting, singing, weeping, and falling prostrate. To be clear, revival is *not* about these manifestations or demonstrative actions. They come with the territory, as it is impossible for people *not* to react when God is touching them. While we should not make a spectacle out of these responses, we should not try to eliminate them, either. When frail humanity collides with this powerful presence of God in our midst, *something* will happen.

The great joy of revival is when the Holy Spirit is so preeminent among the people that conviction seizes the lost and draws them to the cross. We are not trying to convince people to "come to Jesus." The Great Evangelist—the Holy Spirit—powerfully grips sinners and draws them to the Savior. For us to experience this, we *need* God's presence not as some spiritual side item, but as the central focus of all we do in life and ministry. This is exactly why Brownsville had the impact it did. No human can take credit for the work of God in our midst. No program, church, or ministry can stand out as the catalyst in hosting such a powerful outpouring. In the simplest terms, God was in our midst and everything that happened was the supernatural result of His divine movement among us.

You can't predict, work out, or manufacture revival. When the Holy Spirit moves, things can change overnight. I have often wrestled with situations for weeks—sometimes months—trying to get clarity or struggling for a breakthrough in some area of my life.

All it takes is one moment in God's presence to bring solutions. It could be while I am worshipping with a few friends. It could be during a church service. It could be during my private time with the Lord. No matter the context, the common denominator is always the same: God's glory releases supernatural transformation. Perhaps you have experienced this. Maybe you were in bondage to some addiction or habit, but one moment in God's presence brought freedom. His presence brings guidance, clarity, direction, peace, love, a sense of identity, joy, healing, and deliverance.

A REVIVAL OF GOD'S PRESENCE[1]

Revival is directly connected to the visitation of God's powerful presence. It is God stepping down from Heaven and baring His holy arm. He comes and acts and speaks. There is a holy presence and a word on fire. God is in the midst of His people. The Lord is shaking the world. That is revival! It is a time of visitation. If it is confined to one church, it is not revival. If it is confined to the meetings themselves, it is not revival. If it can be traced to the efforts of humanity, it is not revival. If it does not ultimately affect society, it is not revival.

When Jesus was on the earth, He explained to His disciples that it was better for Him to go away so that the Holy Spirit could come. Jesus could only be in one place at one time, but the Holy Spirit could be everywhere. Jesus could directly touch only those who heard and saw Him, but the Holy Spirit could directly touch people anywhere at anytime—even if they were resisting and running. He transcends all human agency!

In revival, the Holy Spirit moves deeply and widely, supernaturally and powerfully. He goes into the homes and schools, into places of business and places of sin, and He brings the sense of the reality of God. He brings conviction! It is impossible to flee from God during revival.

The words of the Lord in Jeremiah 23 and the words of the psalmist in Psalm 139 are always true, but their reality is fully sensed during times of revival:

"Am I only a God nearby," declares the Lord, "and not a God far away?

Who can hide in secret places so that I cannot see them?" declares the Lord.

"Do not I fill heaven and earth?" declares the Lord (Jeremiah 23:23-24 NIV).

Where can I go from your Spirit? Where can I flee from your presence?

If I go up to the heavens, you are there; if I make my bed in the depths, you are there. If I rise on the wings of the dawn, if I settle on the far side of the sea, even there your hand will guide me, your right hand will hold me fast.

If I say, "Surely the darkness will hide me and the light become night around me," even the darkness will not be dark to you; the night will shine like the day, for darkness is as light to you (Psalm 139:7-12 NIV).

STORIES OF DIVINE VISITATION

During the Welsh Revival, it was commonly reported that men would go into the bars to drink, not wanting to go to their homes because they knew their wives were praying and the presence of God was there. But they couldn't escape Him, even in the bars! As they would take the drink in their hands, an unseen hand would stop them, and they would run from that place to their homes and get saved.

As the Spirit converted many of the profane, ungodly coal miners, His presence went with them to work, and they would start their days with prayer and worship. It was said that you could feel His presence in the coal mines as much as you could in church!

Some visitors were once asking for directions to the meetings in one part of Wales. They were told to take the train to such and such a place and get out there. "But how we will know when we are there?" they asked. "You'll feel it!" was the reply. And they did! After getting out of the train, they asked for further directions. They were told to walk to a certain place and turn there. Again they asked, "But how we will know where to turn?" "You'll feel it!" was the answer again. And they did!

That Holy presence is not geographically limited, as Arthur Wallis documented:

> Ships as they drew near the American ports [in 1858] came within a definite zone of heavenly influence. Ship after ship arrived with the same tale of sudden conviction and conversion. In one ship a captain and the entire crew of thirty men found Christ out at sea and entered the harbour rejoicing. Revival broke out on the battleship "North Carolina" through four Christian men who had been meeting in the bowels of the ship for prayer. One evening they were filled with the Spirit and burst into song. Ungodly shipmates who came down to mock were gripped by the power of God, and the laugh of the scornful was soon changed into the cry of the penitent. Many were smitten down, and a gracious work broke out that continued night after night, till they had to send ashore for ministers to help, and the battleship became a Bethel.[2]

I heard a story about a man here in the States who had witnessed to his unsaved friend and prayed for him for years. One day that friend came over to borrow a tool, but no one was home. So he went to the toolshed to find what he was looking for and suddenly the presence of God overtook him. He was convicted of his sins and broke down, putting his faith in Jesus at that very moment.

When he told his Christian friend what had happened to him, he discovered a simple explanation: that faithful believer had prayed with tears for his salvation for a period of years, making intercession for his soul *in that very shed*. The Holy Spirit was there!

Now multiply that picture a thousand times over and spread it across cities, counties, states, and even nations, and you have a glorious picture of revival.

DUNCAN CAMPBELL AND REGIONAL REVIVAL

After the night of prayer in the Hebrides when the house literally shook with the presence of the Lord, Duncan Campbell recalls that:

> The following day when we came to the church we found that the meeting house was already crowded out. A stream of buses had come from the four quarters of the island. Who had told them of the services? I have no way of knowing; God has His own manner of working when men are praying in faith. A butcher's van brought seven men from a distance of seventeen miles.
>
> We gathered in the church, and I spoke for about an hour. The Spirit of God was at work. All over the building men and women were crying for mercy. And on the road outside, I could hear the strong cries of weeping men. I saw both men and women swooning, some falling into

trances. Many were crying, "Oh, God, is there mercy for me?"

A young man beneath the pulpit prayed, "Oh, God, hell is too good for me."

The seven men who came in the butcher's van were all gloriously converted that night.

In the field of evangelism today, the desperate need is for conviction of sin—conviction that will bring men on their faces before God.[3]

When the service was coming to an end and the last people were leaving, the young man by the pulpit, himself a new convert, began to pray, and his prayer lasted for forty-five minutes. Somehow word got out that the meetings were to be held all night! People began to return from all over, packing the church. The service lasted until 4:00 A.M.! But the story doesn't end there. At 4:00 A.M. Campbell received a message:

Mr. Campbell, people are gathered at the Police Station, from the other end of the parish. They are in great distress. Can anyone here come along and pray with them?[4]

Who drew them there? Who convicted them? Many of these people had been strongly opposed to the Gospel right up until that very day. What was happening? The Spirit was at work! This is a true picture of revival:

We went to the Police Station and I shall never forget the scene that met our eyes. Under a starlit sky, with the moon gazing down upon us—and angels, too, I believe, looking over the battlements of glory—were scores of men and women under deep conviction of sin. On the road, by the cottage side, behind a peat stack, they were crying to God for mercy. Yes, the revival had come!

For five weeks this went on. We preached in one church at seven o'clock [in the evening], in another at ten, in a third at twelve, back to the first church at three o'clock [in the morning], then home between five and six, tired, but glad to have found ourselves in the midst of this Heaven-sent movement of the Holy Spirit.[5]

> **In revival, the presence of God was everything to us. It was our oxygen.**

Remarkably, in the first parish where revival hit, Campbell reports that 75 percent of the converts were born again *before* they arrived at the meeting place! There was also an amazing revival among the young people. In those days, not a single young person attended any public worship services in any of the churches, but the very first evening, without announcement or advertisement, the awareness of God *in the dance hall at midnight* became so great that all the young people left there and crowded into the church! And so the revival continued, spreading in like manner to the neighboring counties.[6]

GOD'S PRESENCE MOVING DURING THE BROWNSVILLE REVIVAL

In the same dynamic way that God's presence saturated communities of old, I experienced this firsthand during the Brownsville Revival. Night in and night out, we would go for five, six, or even seven hours in our services. After one evening service had ended, our expectation was already stirred for what God would do *the next night*. Our desire was to be with Him more. In revival, the presence of God was everything to us. It was our oxygen.

Every so often in a service, I felt as though we were just singing songs or going through the motions. It is possible to go through the motions of revival, hoping that our actions alone will sustain God's movement in our community. When I felt this way, I would get on my knees and say, "God, not a service, not *just* another service." It wasn't because of my prayers so much, but the atmosphere would soon change and I would think, "Okay. Praise God, we're heading in the right direction."

Saved Standing in Line

What we saw and experienced during the Brownsville Revival was reminiscent of some of the great revival movements throughout history. Because God's presence was so strong in our midst, there were testimonies of people who got born again simply standing in line outside the church building. The lost would be lined up, waiting for service, and they experienced transformational encounters in God's presence. They got radically and gloriously saved! No preacher. No evangelist. No atmosphere. It was the evangelistic work of the Holy Spirit who was leading them straight to Jesus.

Prayer Meeting Salvation

One of our missionaries who has served for years in the Philippines came to the revival far from God. Some friends had invited him, and he finally attended one of the services. He was a heavy-drinking, lost sinner who was enslaved to addiction. He did not come to a normal church service; he visited Brownsville during the Tuesday night prayer meeting. Picture the environment: The sanctuary was filled with about fifteen hundred people, just praying. At first glance, this would not seem to be the ideal evangelistic service for someone like this. God had other plans, though. Sometimes we get so caught up in our programs that we neglect the ultimate change agent—the presence of the Holy Spirit.

That night, God's presence was so overwhelming that this man was completely undone by the recognition of his sin. He deeply repented before the Lord, wept, and then got gloriously born again, just by encountering the Spirit of God during a prayer meeting. It's God's presence that makes all the difference!

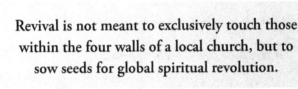

Revival is not meant to exclusively touch those within the four walls of a local church, but to sow seeds for global spiritual revolution.

Electric Baptisms

I remember so many meetings where people would be getting water baptized, and as they shared their stories, the power of God would dramatically fall on them. While giving their testimonies in the baptismal pool, these people would begin to shake and tremble because of God's presence touching them. The whole place would be electrified! Major repentance would suddenly break out as the presence of God filled the church.

As the people in the baptismal testified, the stories they shared about God supernaturally saving, delivering, and restoring their lives released corporate faith and thanksgiving. While celebrating these transformed lives, others would also run to the altar. The baptism testimonies communicated the message loud and clear: If God can deliver me, He can deliver *you, too!*

Transferable Presence

I remember meetings in Italy in May 1998. This was in the midst of the Brownsville Revival. I had been to Italy many times and seen God move, but during these particular meetings we saw the Holy Spirit move powerfully with repentance, with outpouring, and with lives touched in a way that none of us had ever seen. Lifelong missionaries as well as pastors said they had never seen God move like this. Even though we are the same people, there is something about the presence of God in revival that comes with us wherever we go. This is part of the stewardship of revival. Revival is not meant to exclusively touch those within the four walls of a local church, but to sow seeds for global spiritual revolution.

Divine Visitation in the Czech Republic

In the spring of 1996, I traveled to the Czech Republic to minister. We had a service in the afternoon that was just a leaders' retreat with more than one hundred national leaders, husbands and wives together. After I preached, repentance broke out, and leader after leader began to publicly confess sin. I was shocked. I remember being stunned as the wife of a pastor openly confessed to being into pornography. This confession took place in public during an afternoon leaders' retreat! To me, this was a preview of the level of visitation that God had in store for the evening service. What a glorious time it was that night. Worship went on for three and a half hours, and no one could preach because the Spirit of God broke out in an extraordinary way.

The Thunder of God's Presence

This meeting in the Czech Republic took place at a remote location in a small Bible school. Since it did not have adequate room to house everyone, some people were camped outside. This was an annual thing they did—pitch their little tents and camp outside. When the Holy Spirit fell that night, there must have been some type of thunderous roaring sound. In an area pretty distant from the building, one of the wives was with the children, reading to them in their tent. As this roaring became audible, one of the children thought they heard thunder. "Mommy, it's thundering," he said. It was not thundering that day. The other boy said, "No, that's the sound of airplanes flying overhead." But they knew it sounded different. Then one of them said, "That's the sound of drunk people!" This brought it closer to home, as that explanation reflected how the public described the Holy Spirit's outpouring at Pentecost.

WHERE IS GOD'S PRESENCE TODAY?

There are certainly churches and groups that have continued to pursue God's presence. They prize the outpouring of the Holy Spirit and, above all, desire that He is welcome to move in their midst. That's positive. But I would consider this a very, very small minority.

Others are consistently releasing powerful worship songs and have placed a high value on praise and worship. Unfortunately, the very songs that should be catalysts leading us into divine visitation have become tools for Christian entertainment. We sing a set number of songs and are quick to move on to the *next thing*, as if the *next thing* on our agenda is more important than what is on the Holy Spirit's agenda.

Because of the structure many of our churches have embraced and the overall busyness of American life, we often schedule our services so that there is not a lot of room for God to *really* move. This is not to say that having a plan or order of service is wrong;

quite the opposite. Yet within that order, we must make room for the presence of God. While there may be a genuine desire for God to move in our services—particularly in larger congregations—we allow the logistics of running church to prevent us from considering the spontaneous flow of the Spirit.

> **I would rather have the Spirit of God completely charge the atmosphere with His presence than move forward with the best and brightest ministry strategy I've ever conceived.**

I've preached at and worked with many megachurches, and you have *x* number of people to consider. This involves everything from coordinating parking-lot attendants to successfully rotating children's ministry workers on a service-to-service basis. We have become dependent upon so many practical elements, which is understandable, but we may have also become unwilling to consider allowing God to move because His activity might disrupt our smoothly running order of operations. This is true for both large and small churches, as there are examples where God freely moves in both contexts and examples where His Spirit seems to be quenched.

We don't need to have three-hour long services for God to move; we just need hearts that prize His presence above all else. Today many speak of *church culture*. Let it be said that our church culture is marked by a passionate hunger for the Spirit's visitation and outpouring. May that be the defining feature that sets us apart as the Church of Jesus Christ. Not our programs. Not our facilities or buildings. Not our budgets. Not our attendance figures. Not our lights, smoke machines, concerts, guest speakers, or professional praise teams. Contemporary and modern is not our enemy. It is when we assume that all of these secondary matters are *most important* that we run into trouble. We use these things to create an atmosphere for people. I would rather have the Spirit of God completely charge the atmosphere with His presence than move forward with the best and brightest ministry strategy I've ever conceived. My strategies might sound good; but nothing I can devise can ultimately change lives. Even the good ideas I have only work because they were thoughts in God's mind before they were planted in my mind.

This is what I long for across America—people of God who will say, "I *must* encounter God. We *must* have His presence in our midst, and that is more important to us than *anything* else." Everything else will flow from that one desire. The worship will flow from that. The preaching will flow from that. The disciple-making will flow from that. Outreach will flow from that. We must cultivate a hunger and thirst for the presence of God; otherwise when God does come in power, we will not welcome Him and will not be prepared for our day of visitation.

Moses understood this well, confessing to the Lord,

> *If your Presence does not go with us, do not send us up from here. How will anyone know that you are pleased with me and with your people unless you go with us? What else will distinguish me and your people from all the other people on the face of the earth?* (Ex. 33:15-16 NIV)

NOTES

1. Some segments were taken from Dr. Michael Brown's book *From Holy Laughter to Holy Fire* (Shippensburg: Destiny Image, 1996).

2. Cited by Arthur Wallis, *In the Day of Thy Power* (repr., Columbia, MO/Fort Washington, PA: Cityhill/Christian Literature Crusade, 1988), 68.

3. Duncan Campbell, *Revival in the Hebrides*, 7-8.

4. Ibid., 8.

5. Ibid., 8-9.

6. I have these facts from a cassette tape message recorded by Campbell (original date and source unknown).

CHAPTER 13

A REVIVAL OF GOD'S POWER

DR. MICHAEL BROWN

*LORD, I have heard of your fame; I
stand in awe of your deeds, LORD.
Repeat them in our day, in our time make
them known; in wrath remember mercy.*
—HABAKKUK 3:2 NIV

When revival breaks out, we should expect an awakening of God's supernatural power in our midst. This is simply the byproduct of welcoming the presence of the Holy Spirit. There is no divorcing God's presence from His power. Sadly, there are many who seek a powerless revival. We desire an outpouring of the Spirit's conviction to draw sinners to repentance, which is paramount. However, when the same Spirit of God begins to do *more*, touching bodies, healing hearts, restoring minds, and delivering captives from bondage, we get uncomfortable. *This* is one key factor that will either sustain or dissipate a revival: our response to the visitation of God's power. It may not make sense to our natural minds. It may even come in some unexpected packaging. Regardless of our personal preferences, let us endeavor to accommodate what God is doing and celebrate the outpouring of His power!

HEALINGS, MIRACLES, AND DELIVERANCE IN GOD'S PRESENCE

During the Brownsville Revival, we wholeheartedly welcomed the move of God's Spirit through signs, wonders, miracles, and deliverances. That said, they were not front and center. They were simply celebrated by-products of His manifest presence in our midst that reflect what the New Testament faith looks like when demonstrated.

> When revival breaks out, we should expect an awakening of God's supernatural power in our midst.

Deliverance

Outside of conversions and recommitments to Christ, deliverance was a key part of what the Holy Spirit was doing in revival. It is a component of salvation—an expression of being set free from sin and an integral element of the repentance process. As people gave their lives to Christ, they weren't simply saying, "God, I accept You on my terms." This is the counterfeit Christianity that so many espouse today. When people gave their hearts to Jesus during revival, they were not signing up to be part of a spiritual club; they were desperate to leave the old behind and fully embrace the new life that Jesus had for them. In God's presence, they tasted something infinitely superior to the life of sin, bondage, and addiction they were leaving behind. Conversion was often accompanied by (or shortly followed up with) deliverance. People would get saved... and then they got "un-slaved" from the different shackles that prevented them from experiencing God's abundant life.

Divine Healing

There was less emphasis placed on physical healing; not because we denied its importance but mainly because the burden Steve Hill was carrying was evangelistic in nature. He was compelled to see the lost come to Christ and the prodigals come home. He did not preach on supernatural healing or miracles, and yet they still happened. Again, *when God's presence comes, He does not leave His power behind.*

We would regularly hear testimonies of people being miraculously healed. Even though it was not an area we majored on, we still considered it a healthy part of God's movement in our midst. I welcome healing, embrace it, and see it as absolutely the New Testament, Kingdom of God normal. It is also a dynamic part of the Spirit's outpouring around the world.

Accidental Miracles

Many times, we prayed for people without knowing what was going on in their lives. These prayers released an "accidental" healing. We were not identifying people with physical infirmities, sickness, and disease, calling them forward, and praying specifically for those needs. Again, I welcome this and place a high value on the ministry of healing because it is a key sign of the Kingdom's in-breaking. This simply was not the focus of the Brownsville

Revival. Yet in the midst of preaching repentance and praying for those hungry for a fresh touch of God in their lives, people were accidentally healed—and some from major diseases. I don't know how else to describe it. It was accidental to us, maybe, but quite intentional from God's vantage point.

Overwhelmed by God's Power

Of course, there was the manifestation of God's power that people refer to as being "slain in the spirit." This did not often happen in the way you would think. I am talking about praying for some hulking guy, maybe six foot five, three hundred and twenty pounds—a real brute of a guy who was a college football player—who was standing with his arms crossed, looking at us skeptically. The people gathered around him kept saying, "Pray for him. Pray for him!" We knew it was a touch from God when we barely reached out a finger to touch him and the next thing we knew he was laid out on the ground, shaking, weeping, and encountering God. You can't manufacture that.

> **The ultimate question is not whether people were touched and fell down, but whether they lived a transformed life *after* they got up.**

Touched or Transformed?

The big issue for us was *not* whether people cried, shook, fell, or experienced some kind of physical manifestation. These are quite neutral in the scheme of revival. We place too much emphasis on them to the positive *and* negative. To the positive, we tend to exalt the manifestations above the presence of the Messiah, and to the negative, we are so disparaging toward *any* demonstration of God's power that we shut down the service if things start to get a little uncomfortable. We achieve balance when we keep everything in perspective. The ultimate question is not whether people were touched and fell down, but whether they lived a transformed life *after* getting up from the floor. Any encounter with God, regardless of the manifestations, that produces a sustained passion and wholehearted surrender to Jesus in someone's life is certainly worth praising God for.

Often, the dynamic encounters that produced different manifestations showed people that God was real and that He was near. These were often dramatic touches that ultimately led to deep conversions and miraculous transformations.

WHATEVER HAPPENED TO THE POWER OF GOD?[1]

I am absolutely convinced that the Church of today is not fully experiencing what Jesus died for and not yet becoming what He prayed for. There is something infinitely more and completely other than what we are walking in today. There is a power, a purity, an authority, an anointing, a glory we have barely touched. The Lord is coming for a beautiful bride. There is much preparation, restoration, and reformation still to take place.

Jesus taught that "whoever wants to save his life will lose it, but whoever loses his life for Me will find it" (Matt. 16:25 NIV). He is the pearl of great price. "What good will it be for someone to gain the whole world, yet forfeit their soul? Or what can anyone give in exchange for their soul? For the Son of Man is going to come in his Father's glory with his angels, and then he will reward each person according to what they have done" (Matt. 16:26-27 NIV). This calls for total reorientation. This calls for new priorities and purposes. Our lives are not our own. We will give an account.

Paul was a man possessed by the living God:

I have been crucified with Christ and I no longer live, but Christ lives in me. The life I now live in the body, I live by faith in the Son of God, who loved me and gave himself for me (Galatians 2:20 NIV).

He bore on his body the very marks of the Lord (see Gal. 6:17). He was branded a disciple for life.

But this call to total surrender and radical commitment is not just for the super saints. All of us were "buried with him through baptism into death in order that, just as Christ was raised from the dead through the glory of the Father, we too may live a new life" (Rom. 6:4 NIV). The old ways should be a thing of the past:

For [we] died, and [our] life is now hidden with Christ in God...[so] our citizenship is in heaven. And we eagerly await a Savior from there, the Lord Jesus Christ, who, by the power that enables him to bring everything under his control, will transform our lowly bodies so that they will be like his glorious body (Colossians 3:3, Philippians 3:20-21 NIV).

That is a vision worth living for. That is a hope worth dying for. That is the goal of our faith. That is the future we await.

There is much glory in store for God's people, but it is not just reserved for the world to come! There is a glory for the saints in this life, but we must set a new course if we are to see it in our day. We must be honest with ourselves.

The road before us is difficult, and the task before us demanding. There are many hard questions to be asked and much soul-searching to be done. Some of the answers are painful and disturbing. Some of the revelations are unnerving and alarming. But do we really have any choice? Can we continue to go on with the show? How much more disappointment can we bear? Will we allow our generation to come and go, bequeathing only frustration to our children?

> There is much glory in store for God's people, but it is not just reserved for the world to come! There is a glory for the saints in this life, but we must set a new course if we are to see it in our day.

We must follow the path of truth wherever it takes us. We must keep our eyes fixed on our Almighty Lord and our hearts fixed firmly on His faithful love. He will not let us down. "His dominion is an everlasting dominion that will not pass away, and his kingdom is one that will never be destroyed" (Dan. 7:14 NIV). He will have His ultimate way on the earth. Can He have His way in you and me?

Revival *must* take God's power outside the building, beyond the confines of our Christian gatherings. This is the only hope for revolution in the world. If the way we live outside the building is not characterized by holiness and sacrificial love for the Lord and the lost, *that is not revival*. And if everything that happens in our revival meetings comes through the hands of human vessels—without the supernatural visitations outside the church, without the abiding presence, without the clear evidence that God Himself has "stepped down from heaven" in power—*that is not revival*.[2]

It's time to begin the journey back to His standard of normal. Therein lies the *true* power of God in demonstration!

Restore Your glory, O Lord!

NOTES

1. Adapted from Dr. Michael Brown's book *Whatever Happened to the Power of God?*

2. Adapted from Dr. Michael Brown's book *From Holy Laughter to Holy Fire.*

CHAPTER 14

THE KEY THAT UNLOCKS REVIVAL: REPENTANCE

DR. MICHAEL BROWN

Man is born with his face turned away from God.
When he truly repents, he is turned right
round toward God; he leaves his old life.
—D. L. MOODY

We cannot have true revival without deep repentance. The great moves of God's Spirit throughout history have all come accompanied by deep conviction of sin and repentance. When the authentic presence of God touches us, we become aware of His holiness and our utter inability to stand before Him apart from the redemptive work of Christ.

There is hardly anything more fundamental to the life of a believer than repentance—hardly anything more life-giving, more liberating, more glorious. That's why the devil has sought to discredit it.

THERE CAN BE NO REVIVAL WITHOUT TRUE REPENTANCE

There can be no possible return to God without repentance. Repentance speaks of turning back. The notion that repentance is merely a change of mind is a deficient definition. It is a change of mind and heart and life. It is a deliberate turning away from that which is wrong and destructive and a turning back to God and His mercy.

If I am heading north when I am supposed to be heading south, if I don't turn around, I will never get back to where I need to be. This is exactly what repentance is—an about-face. Repentance is recognizing that something is terribly wrong. Repentance honestly acknowledges something *dead* that needs reviving.

We cannot have true revival without deep repentance.

Consider this illustration. If I were a medical doctor who had not been very sharp in his diagnosis, watching people who were sick or even dying because of my misdiagnoses would be terribly painful. Spiritually, we have done this level of disservice to the body of Christ. Many leaders have done such a disservice to their own churches by not being the men and women God has called them to be. We resist preaching sin and repentance because they are not popular. The problem is that when we refrain from telling people *what they need to hear*, we spiritually misdiagnose the dying.

In Acts 3:19-20, Peter tells his Jewish listeners, "Repent therefore, and turn back, that your sins may be blotted out, that times of refreshing may come from the presence of the Lord." Repentance is what opens the door to blessing, revival, and renewal. This is why past revivalists, such as Frank Bartleman, have stated that "the depth of revival is determined by the depth of the spirit of repentance that is obtained."

People might attempt to experience revival *without* repentance. As such, they want God to put icing on the cake of their custom-made Christianity. They are essentially saying, "God, we want more, so give us more of You without us having to face the fact that we are going in the wrong direction." This is a false idea of revival, as we are essentially asking God to bless our sinfulness. We want to live in the sinful state we are presently in, but we desire the blessings of God to flow in our lives. We cannot have it both ways. We can't head south when we are supposed to be going north and expect God to bless the *wrong journey*. That's problematic. It just won't happen.

In the following pages, I share a Scriptural understanding of repentance.[1] I also get very practical and give you a biblical blueprint on *how* to repent. This is not intended to be a works-oriented formula that brings some kind of burden to your walk with the Lord. The problem is that since we have neglected this key component of the Christian life for so long, we don't have a clear vision of what repentance looks like when fleshed out in our lives.

WHAT IS TRUE REPENTANCE?

Mention repentance to most believers and immediately they think of condemnation, browbeating, negativity, judgment, and death. Nothing could be further from the truth. Repentance is a gift from God. Without it, sinners cannot be regenerated and saints cannot be renewed. It is a wonder of God's infinite grace. Only the imperfect are candidates for it.

Repentance is exclusively for those who have fallen short, who acknowledge their need, who have turned away, who have sinned, who want to come back. It is not for the totally righteous or self-sufficient. They do not qualify for such a precious gem! Nor do they know what they are missing.

Repentance is God's activating grace. It remakes and restores and repairs. It is the essential step to redemption. It starts in darkness and ends in light. It starts in bondage and ends in freedom. It starts in death and ends in life. It makes the unclean clean and the unholy holy. It makes the difference between Heaven and Hell. God only forgives those who repent.

True repentance, the fruit of godly sorrow, "leads to salvation and leaves no regret" (2 Cor. 7:10 NIV). God's heavenly Kingdom is filled with repentant sons and daughters of Adam—those who have sorrowed for their sins and found pardon. They will never sorrow again.

> **Repentance is a gift from God. Without it, sinners cannot be regenerated and saints cannot be renewed.**

John Milton was right when he described repentance as "the golden key that opens the palace of eternity." Yet the gates of God's Kingdom are shut to those who refuse to repent. They can never enter. They must do without salvation, and they will have much to regret. They cast off godly sorrow in this life, and they will have the sorrow of this world in the life to come. How tragic!

We cannot afford to pass over repentance. Repentance is the most basic of the basics, the very first of "the elementary teachings about Christ" (Heb. 6:1 NIV). It is the special property of the human race.

Of all God's creation, only humans can repent.

REPENT AND REJOICE!

Of all God's creation, only humans can repent. That's why "there is rejoicing in the presence of the angels of God over one sinner who repents" (Luke 15:10 NIV). It is a thrilling sight for them to behold! That's why the early believers, all of them Jews, praised God, because He had granted even to Gentiles "repentance that leads to life" (Acts 11:18). This was their way into the inheritance. In fact, one reason Jesus has not yet returned is this: He is waiting for more people to repent!

First, David appealed for mercy, pure and simple in Psalm 51. "Have mercy on me, O God, according to your unfailing love."

Then he cast himself wholly on the goodness of God. He dove into the ocean of grace: "According to Your great compassion, blot out my transgressions" (Ps. 51:1 NIV).

It is repent or perish. Repentance means being saved from our sins. The Scriptures speak of "repentance unto life" and "repentance unto salvation." There is nothing negative about that! Repentance is only for those the Lord has not rejected: "Those whom I love I rebuke and discipline. So be earnest, and repent. Here I am! I stand at the door and knock" (Rev. 3:19-20 NIV). Praise God when

He knocks at our door! We will experience mercy and grace if we humble ourselves and repent.

DAVID'S JOURNEY TO REPENTANCE

Look how David responded when Nathan the prophet exposed the king's sin. This is the first step to repentance—having our sin laid open and brought to light. Who wants to have cancer in his spirit and not even know about it? Thank God when uncleanness is revealed!

First David appealed for mercy, pure and simple.

> *Have mercy on me, O God, according to Your unfailing love." He cast Himself wholly on the goodness of God. He dove into the ocean of grace: "According to Your great compassion, blot out my transgressions* (Psalm 51:1 NIV).

What a fantastic request! David comes with his transgressions, his iniquity, and his sin. He is filthy and vile and stained. Yet he appeals to his holy God's unfailing love and great compassion. And the Lord is pleased with this! He invites it; He welcomes it; He desires it. He wants to make us whole. He doesn't want to hide His face from us. He wants to hide His face from our sin.

> *Who is a God like you, who pardons sins and forgives the transgression of the remnant of his inheritance? You do not stay angry forever* [hallelujah!] *but delight to show mercy.* [Read this again: God delights to show mercy!] *You will again have compassion on us; you will tread our sins underfoot and hurl all our iniquities into the depths of the sea* (Micah 7:18-19 NIV)

This is the God we approach!

Look at the boldness of David's repentance. The man who committed adultery and arranged for cold-blooded murder—the one who disappointed and offended the Lord—now asks that his evil be blotted out and washed away, that he be cleansed until he is whiter than snow, that gladness and rejoicing be restored to him, that God create for him a pure heart and renew a steadfast spirit within him, and that the Lord open his lips so that his tongue could sing God's righteousness and his mouth declare God's praise. (See Psalm 51.) Amazing!

What an incredible exchange! David comes with iniquity; he leaves with purity. He comes with guilt; he leaves with pardon. He comes weighed down; he leaves rejoicing. We serve a compassionate God!

THE COST OF REPENTANCE

Repentance is not cheap. It cost Jesus His lifeblood. It brought Him down to the depths. He paid the price to ransom our lives. He suffered so that we might be changed: "He himself bore our sins in his body on the tree, so that we might die to sin and live to righteousness" (1 Pet. 2:24).

Repentance is where it begins. We die to the old and embrace the new; we turn from the world and turn to the Lord. It is rebirth; it is salvation; it is new life. If we continue to live as we did before, then we should question our salvation—and question our repentance.

Jesus did not die in vain.

While speaking of His disciples, the Lord said, "For them I sanctify Myself, that they too may be truly sanctified" (John 17:19 NIV). He set Himself apart to His Father—every second of every day He lived on this earth—so that we would be set apart, too. "Both the one who makes men holy and those who are made holy are of the same family. So Jesus is not ashamed to call them brothers" (Heb. 2:11 NIV). His Father is our Father, too.

John taught us that "Everyone who sins breaks the law." But Jesus "appeared so that he might take away our sins. And in him is no sin." Therefore "no one who lives in him keeps on sinning. No one who continues to sin has either seen him or known him" (1 John 3:4-6 NIV).

Could anything be clearer? "The one who does what is sinful is of the devil." But "the reason the Son of God appeared was to destroy the devil's work." Therefore "no one who is born of God will continue to sin, because God's seed remains in them; they cannot go on sinning, because they have been born of God" (1 John 3:8-9 NIV). Whoever has been born of God has received a new nature. The core of his being is different. It is conversion in the truest sense of the word. Conversion means revolution and change.

The Roman believers used to be slaves to sin. "But now that you have been set free from sin and have become slaves of God, the fruit you get leads to sanctification and its end, eternal life" (Rom. 6:22). They were no longer the same. The Corinthians were once guilty of every kind of vice, but not anymore! "You were washed, you were sanctified, you were justified in the name of the Lord Jesus Christ and by the Spirit of our God" (1 Cor. 6:11). They were not even to eat with so-called believers who walked in the old ways of the flesh. The days of gross sin were behind them. To the Ephesians it was written: "For at one time you were darkness, but now you are light in the Lord" (Eph. 5:8).

There was no way around the simple facts. The saved were to be as different from the unsaved as day is from night.

This is the message we have heard from him and proclaim to you, that God is light, and in him is no darkness at all. If we say we have fellowship with him while we walk in darkness, we lie and do not practice the truth. But if we walk in the light, as he is in the light, we have fellowship with one another, and the blood of Jesus his Son cleanses us from all sin (1 John 1:5-7).

There is no middle ground. Paul reminded Titus:

For we ourselves were once foolish, disobedient, led astray, slaves to various passions and pleasures, passing our days in malice and envy, hated by others and hating one another. But when the goodness and loving kindness of God our Savior appeared, he saved us, not because of works done by us in righteousness, but according to his own mercy, by the washing of regeneration and renewal of the Holy Spirit (Titus 3:3-5).

What a glorious transformation! This is what we must do in order to see such radical change. The same rule applies for sinner and saint.

THE JOURNEY OF REPENTANCE

We must follow the example of David:

We must fully accept our guilt. "For I know my transgressions, and my sin is always before me."

We must acknowledge that we have offended God. "Against you, you only have I sinned and done what is evil in your sight."

We must declare that God is completely blameless. "So you are right in your verdict and justified when you judge."

We must renounce all claims to righteousness on our own. "Surely I was sinful at birth, sinful from the time my mother conceived me."

We must commit ourselves to abandon sin and pursue the Lord. "Then will I teach transgressors your ways, so that sinners will turn back to you."

We must humble ourselves before our Maker. "My sacrifice, O God, is a broken spirit; a broken and contrite heart you, God, will not despise."

We must ask for and expect mercy. "Have mercy on me, O God, according to your unfailing love." This is the essence of the entire psalm! (See Psalm 51 NIV.)

True repentance says,

> *God, You are right and I am wrong. You have not failed me, I have failed You. I deserve Your judgment, and You would be completely justified in pouring out Your anger on me. But instead, in meekness and reverence, I ask You to be merciful to me, to cleanse me and make me whole, to turn my heart and renew my mind, to give me the grace to obey so that I may never go this way again, according to Your abundant kindness! Lord, I forsake my sin.*

Repentance sets the prisoners free.

True repentance will always bear much fruit. A truly repentant person will have no objection to having his repentance tested. If he is a leader who has seriously fallen, he will gratefully submit to discipline and rehabilitation, for the truly repentant man is humble, not contentious. He is blessed just to know he is forgiven and accepted. He will take all necessary steps to regain people's respect. He knows bearing fruit can take time.

This is how it should be with the brand-new believer, too. Anyone who has truly been saved in the biblical sense of the word will not continue to live the old life once he becomes aware that it is sin. He belongs to a new master now! He will be teachable and hungry for instruction. After all, he should be joyful beyond words if he has truly repented and become a child of the King, if he realizes that God Almighty has received him and that he has received eternal life. Salvation for the lost through repentance and faith is a quality transaction. And deliverance for the bound-up believer through repentance and faith is also a lasting event.

Unfortunately, many of God's people have failed to distinguish between repentance (a gift from God that produces lasting change) and remorse (a human feeling that never moves beyond guilt and regret). They live in bondage for years, although they "repent" dozens and dozens of times. Repentance sets the prisoners free. "If the Son sets you free, you will be free indeed" (John 8:36).

How about you? Are you walking in freedom or in futility? True repentance delivers you *from* bondage—it does not bring you back *into* it.

NOTE

1. Segment adapted from Dr. Michael Brown's book *Whatever Happened to the Power of God*.

PART FOUR

KEYS TO SUSTAINING A LIFE OF REVIVAL

This final section and its corresponding chapters are divided into a slightly different format than the previous segments. Each key has its own separate chapter. These are devotional in nature and give you some practical ways to sustain a lifestyle of personal revival. It is what happens *after* your encounter with God that determines how you will live the rest of your Christian life.

Press in and access everything the Holy Spirit has made available!

> *The tragedy is that many of us are living desperate*
> *Christian life. Sunday comes and we get some*
> *strength, and then we lose some on Monday; a*
> *good deal is gone by Tuesday and we wonder*
> *whether we have anything left. On Wednesday*

it has all gone and then we exist. Or perhaps refreshment comes in some other way, some meeting we attend, some friends we meet. Now that is the old order of things, that is not the new. He puts a well within us. We are not always drawing from somewhere outside. The well, the spring, goes on springing up from within into everlasting life.
—Martyn Lloyd-Jones

There is no question that God works, often powerfully, in the old structures. But it is inevitable that those very structures put serious limitations on His working. It is all too easy for the ground gained to be lost, for the situation to revert, and for the whole process to need repeating within a short space of time. Take the 1950, Lewis Awakening. Though confined to certain Presbyterian churches in the Outer Hebrides, this was a powerful movement of the Spirit that deeply affected those communities at the time. Many found faith in Christ, and some of these are now in full-time service. But the fact remains that in less than a decade you could visit those very churches where God had worked so powerfully and never suspect that they had ever tasted revival. Without a change of structure it is virtually impossible to conserve the fruits of revival.
—Arthur Wallis

A true revival means nothing less than a revolution, casting out the spirit of worldliness and selfishness, and making God and His love triumph in the heart and life.
—Andrew Murray

CHAPTER 15

EMBRACE A GOD-CENTERED PERSPECTIVE

DR. MICHAEL BROWN

*To seek the fulfillment of ourselves in God—that
is, to seek only the blessings and refreshing of
God, but not seek God for himself—this type of
spirituality is the enemy of the cross of Christ.*
—St. John of the Cross

To live a *revival lifestyle*, we need to recognize that everything starts with God, not us. He doesn't exist to please us. Heaven does *not* revolve around God making us healthy, wealthy, and comfortable. God Almighty is not our butler or bellhop. The Spirit of God is most welcome in a life where the *fear of the Lord* is present.

When we have a healthy, biblical awe of God, it confirms that we are embracing a biblical perspective of the faith.

We need to start with God and *not* with ourselves. We need to get back to a biblical basis of the faith, which is that we are here to please Him. Remember, "all things were created through him and for him" (Col. 1:16). Our world revolves around Him, not the other way around. Here's the balance: Because of Jesus, we don't work to please God; we work *because* God is pleased. We could never work hard enough to become pleasing or acceptable to the Holy God. Impossible. But because of Jesus's redemptive work on the cross, we *live* responsively. When we live *in full view of God's mercies*, constantly remembering what Jesus has done on our behalf, to give the rest of our lives to "please" Him is a sacrifice, yes, but one that our hearts burn to make (see Rom. 12:1). *This* is what it means to live a revival lifestyle.

> **The grace that God gives you is grace that comes with responsibility.**

In our modern Christian culture, it seems as though we have figured out ways to compartmentalize God so He fits into our busy schedules. There are soccer moms, busy dads—the whole bit. I'm not at all belittling family schedules. Life can be very hectic and very full. At the same time, God must be more valuable to us than *anything*. We must put God first as opposed to just trying to to squeeze Him into our lives. This perspective impacts everything. Now we have the quick and easy forty-five-minute Sunday service. That's a good one to get to because we are in and out fast. Culturally, it seems as though this is how we look at God as a whole.

Stop and reflect on the fact that Jesus died for us in *our entirety*, and therefore our reasonable service is to give ourselves entirely back to Him. It's not coercion. By no means am I trying to encourage strict religious formalism. When we truly see Him for who He is and what He has done—when we live with a fixed gaze upon the cross—everything changes. Our hearts should passionately burn to live lives that are ever offering up heartfelt thank-yous to the Lamb of God.

We also need to recognize the power of worldliness and turn from it. Revival will never be sustained by those who attempt the balancing act of keeping one foot in the world while striving to keep the other in the Kingdom. This allowance for compromise demonstrates that our hearts are not truly burning for Jesus. We need to turn away from carnality and compromise and ask God to show us what it means to live for Him alone. We need to pray, "Lord, show us what it means to be holy." Again, this is not a matter of obtaining God's favor through our good performance; it is a matter of walking worthy of the Lord. John writes that "everyone who thus hopes in him purifies himself as he is pure" (1 John 3:3). The One who called us is pure. The Spirit within us is holy.

Jesus's blood brought you and me into a right standing with God that we could never obtain by our own merits (see 2 Cor. 5:21). We are declared righteous before the Holy God because of Jesus, even though we don't always live in perfect righteousness. But we are called to walk that righteousness out, to walk worthy of the Lord. Because we stand righteous in His sight, we desire to reflect this righteousness in our everyday lives. This is sanctification. Remember, the grace that God gives you is grace that comes with responsibility. It is grace that supernaturally placed us into right standing with God, *and* it is the same grace that empowers us to live out this new identity!

CHAPTER 16

GET DESPERATE ENOUGH

PASTOR JOHN KILPATRICK

The key to Christian living is a
thirst and hunger for God.
—JOHN PIPER

When you see desperation rise up in somebody, you know they're not going to stop until they get what they are desperate for. They're not going to settle for politics. They're not going to settle for goose bumps. They're not going to settle for a nice sermon or a good worship. They're not going to settle for *anything* until they touch God and have an encounter with Him. It's the deep part of your spirit crying out to that deeper place in God. That's desperation.

What do hungry people look like? The signs are clear. You can see their ribs, their hair turns yellow, and their eyes sink back into their heads. Food is the only solution. When you see people who are clearly malnourished, you know they've got to have nutrition. When you see people today who are hungry for God, they are spiritually malnourished, and you can see it on them. They're thin. They're weak and they're desperate. How hungry are you?

If you get desperate enough, you'll pay any price. A parent who is desperate to see their child receive medical help will go to any length. They will visit any city, borrow money, and go to any specialist to make sure their child receives the best care.

If you're desperate enough, you will go catch a flight to Hong Kong; you'll catch a flight to Africa; you'll catch a flight to Brownsville. No price is too great. No inconvenience is too overpowering. You're desperate, and you're going to get what you need from God, period.

If you're desperate enough, you will go *any place* where the manifest presence of God authentically moves in power. When you know that the glory of God is somewhere and that people are being touched, your spirit starts burning. "I've got to go," you think. It's not something people are pressuring you to do; your spirit drives you toward it. Something is drawing you toward that powerful presence of God.

If you get desperate enough, you'll pay any price.

What if you heard right now that God was moving powerfully in Durban, South Africa? Baton Rogue, Louisiana? London, England? How hungry are you to encounter His presence? Some argue,

"You don't need to go somewhere to experience God." I've heard others say, "God knows where to find me if He wants to encounter me." These perspectives disqualify us from His powerful touch. What we value, we pursue. Our self-effort is an expression of worship to God. It's not works based; it's passion fueled. We *do* what we are passionate about. If we are genuinely desperate to experience God and have His Spirit satisfy our soul's deep hunger, we will do anything and go anywhere.

You see, I know what He did at Brownsville. I know what He has done in other places. I'm going where He is moving. I'm going to be in His presence. I'm going to experience His power. There's something about being in God's manifest presence that supernaturally changes you. So many today are looking for quick fixes and spiritual self-improvement. The key to transformation is not found in the latest gimmicks; it's found in the glory of God. Once we taste of His pure presence, we will never be satisfied with the dross of the world again.

Paul recognized this, explaining, "But we all, with unveiled face, beholding as in a mirror the glory of the Lord, are being transformed into the same image from glory to glory, just as by the Spirit of the Lord" (2 Cor. 3:18 NKJV).

CHAPTER 17

WHEN GOD MOVES, ACCEPT HIS INVITATION

PASTOR JOHN KILPATRICK

When it is a question of God's almighty
Spirit, never say, "I can't."
—OSWALD CHAMBERS

God is looking for people and communities He can pour His Spirit into. Scripture tells us that "the eyes of Yahweh roam throughout the earth to show Himself strong for those whose hearts are completely His" (2 Chron. 16:9 HCSB). There is a specific posture of the heart that qualifies us to be carriers of revival.

Here is an Old Testament story that perfectly illustrates how God qualifies people for revival. In Second Kings 4, we read the following account of the Shunammite's son:

When the child had grown, he went out one day to his father among the reapers. And he said to his father, "Oh, my head, my head!" The father said to his servant, "Carry him to his mother." And when he had lifted him and brought him to his mother, the child sat on her lap till noon, and then he died. And she went up and laid him on the bed of the man of God and shut the door behind him and went out (2 Kings 4:18-21).

Scripture records that when the son died, his mother laid him "on the bed of the man of God." She immediately set out to find Elisha, who was at Mount Carmel (verses 22-25).

When the man of God saw her coming, he said to Gehazi his servant, "Look, there is the Shunammite. Run at once to meet her and say to her, 'Is all well with you? Is all well with your husband? Is all well with the child?'" And she answered, "All is well." (2 Kings 4:25-26).

This was not the truth; her son was dead. When she spoke to Elisha, she told him a different story:

And when she came to the mountain to the man of God, she caught hold of his feet. And Gehazi came to push her away. But the man of God said, "Leave her alone, for she is in bitter distress (2 Kings 4:27).

She was in a desperate situation. In response, Elisha and his servant, Gehazi, followed her back to the dead child. They arrived back at her house and Elisha saw the boy "lying dead on his bed" (2 Kings 4:32).

Here is a classic illustration of revival. The biblical account states that Elisha drew near to the dead boy and "went up and lay on the child, putting his mouth on his mouth, his eyes on his eyes, and his hands on his hands" (2 Kings 4:34).

Hands represent healing, eyes represent vision, and the mouth represents the prophetic. As Elisha stretched himself out on the boy, the Bible says he *did not* resurrect the child from the dead. Note what Elisha does and what happens in response.

And as he stretched himself upon him, the flesh of the child became warm. Then he got up again and walked once back and forth in the house, and went up and stretched himself upon him (2 Kings 4:34-35).

Ultimately Elisha *did* raise the boy from the dead. However, it was not an instant resurrection. By stretching his body over the boy, Elisha did not immediately resurrect him. Instead he *warmed* the boy up. Elisha got up off the boy after he warmed up his flesh and walked around the room.

How we respond to the Spirit's warming determines if we are fit to carry the fires of revival.

This story is a fitting illustration of how the Holy Spirit can extend His invitation for revival. The Spirit's presence "warms" up churches. If the church is dead and the pastor is praying for revival, the Holy Spirit will stretch out upon the church and warm things up with the fire of God. He does not instantly bring the full resurrection power of revival. Instead, the Spirit broods over the community, evaluating how the people respond. The warming is His divine invitation to revival. Remember, God is looking for hearts that willingly respond to His movement. He desires to show

Himself strong to those who are willing to embrace His manifest presence in their midst.

How we respond to any trace of the Spirit's movement in our lives and our communities is essential. If we desire the fire of God to fall, we must first welcome the Spirit's warming. This is where things get very real between God and us. We may be praying for revival, but if we shut down the warming of the Spirit, we are not fit to carry revival. It's that simple. This says, "God, I want revival, but only on my own terms."

The Holy Spirit watches to see how we receive the "warm up." He listens to hear if the pastor is saying, "Well, I don't think sister so-and-so likes what's going on at the church. I don't think brother so-and-so is happy with the direction we are headed in. I saw them leaving, and I don't think they liked this move of God thing." Perhaps the Spirit hears, "We're going to have to be really careful how we handle this presence of the Holy Spirit stuff." Maybe a board member says to the pastor, "You know, Pastor, until we started having strange services like this, we were just getting doctors, lawyers, and all kinds of elite, specialist people at the church. If this kind of thing continues, we're going to lose these people because they're not going to put up with this." I repeat, how we respond to the Spirit's warming determines if we are fit to carry the fires of revival.

This is where we are faced with a choice as leaders and as individuals. As leaders, we must say yes to God no matter what the cost. As followers of Jesus, we must say yes no matter how unusual and uncomfortable things are. Jesus is renowned for inviting people into uncomfortable places. Comfort is not His concern for you or me; it's Christ-likeness. He wants you and me transformed to greater reflect His nature to the world. This happens in the glory. This happens when our eyes are privileged to witness the authentic power of God in action. It may be different than what we grew up with. It might be unusual when measured next to our spiritual background. At the day's end, our heritage and background are both at the mercy of God's Word. If Scripture tells us one thing, and our past tells us another, we go with God's Word no matter what. It's plain and simple.

If the Spirit moves in your life and church with gifts of healing, wonders, miracles, deep conviction of sin, repentance, groans, cries, falling, and so on, don't be distracted by how uncomfortable *you feel*. In many ways, these phenomena were new and unusual for me during Brownsville—and theologically, I claimed to believe in all of it! The question is not *what do you believe?* The real question is *how will you welcome the Holy Spirit when He starts moving?* It's easy to discuss theology because it distances us somewhat from reality. We can study the movement of the Holy Spirit, but when it starts to happen in our lives or our communities, what's "in print" starts to take place before our eyes.

How will you respond?

CHAPTER 18

DON'T DIE BESIDE THE ARK

LARRY SPARKS

God is looking for a people who are ready to accommodate a visitation of His glory in their midst—no matter what it costs. Popularity. Prominence. Power. Notoriety. Reputation. When we measure these things beside the possibility of experiencing a visitation of God's presence, they must all fall miserably short. This is essential in order for our prayers for revival to prevail.

A NEW DEMONSTRATION OF CHRISTIANITY

I want us to consider some of the things that prevent us from going full force after revival in our lives and churches. There is no room for halfhearted effort when it comes to our desperate cry for the move of God. When I say *desperate* or use the term *desperation*, I am not implying that we are trying to twist God's arm or coerce

Him to send an outpouring of the Spirit. Desperation does not seek to change God from being unwilling to willing. He is not clenching His fist around revival, looking to send it down to the person who begs, barters, and pleads long enough. Not at all. Rather, it's desperation to align our hearts with the Father's. This prayer is not about begging God to open Heaven. Instead, it is asking the Holy Spirit to help us steward the open Heaven we have already received because of Pentecost.

> **God is looking for a people who are ready to accommodate a visitation of His glory in their midst—no matter what it costs.**

God not only wants to send revival; He wants us to receive the invitation that revival extends, make the appropriate adjustments, and live out a whole new expression of Christianity. This is what the world is in dire need of. Revivalist Leonard Ravenhill said it best: "The world outside there is not waiting for a new definition of Christianity, it's waiting for a new demonstration of Christianity."

If we desire for our homes, churches, communities, and nations to live under an open Heaven, we must pray like there is nothing more important to us than welcoming the move of God with open arms.

COMPROMISE THAT UNPLUGS OUR PRAYERS

When we compromise on our definition of revival, we are essentially pulling the plug on our prayers. We are removing them from their power source. To pray with effectiveness, there must be an element of strong belief. We might claim to have faith for revival, but ultimately it is revival with strings attached. This will not suffice.

The compromise I am specifically addressing is the desire to have a people-pleasing revival. This is historically and fundamentally impossible. We can use all the revival language we want in our services, books, and conferences. We can hold all-night revival prayer meetings. No matter how intense our efforts, if ultimately we have an agenda in our heart to "steady the ox cart," we are not fit to host God's glory. Consider this account in Scripture for a moment:

And David and all the house of Israel were celebrating before the Lord, with songs and lyres and harps and tambourines and castanets and cymbals. And when they came to the threshing floor of Nacon, Uzzah put out his hand to the ark of God and took hold of it, for the oxen stumbled. And the anger of the Lord was kindled against Uzzah, and God struck him down there because of his error, and he died there beside the ark of God (2 Samuel 6:5-7).

In Second Samuel 6:5-7, we see what happens when man makes any attempt to "steady" the presence of God. Everything was set for the day to be glorious. The Ark of the Covenant had been recaptured from the Philistines, and now there was a great procession heralding the return of God's presence among the people. For our purposes, it is worth noting that Uzzah's sin was taking hold of the Ark when the ox stumbled (see verse 6). The Message Bible translates verse 7 in an interesting way, perhaps bringing more clarity to the severity of God's judgment upon Uzzah. We read that "God blazed in anger against Uzzah and struck him hard because he had profaned the Chest."

When it comes to Old Testament accounts like this, we cannot assume to draw prophetic parallels between this story and New

Testament realities. While these passages may not be prophetic in nature, I am convinced they are illustrative. They reveal a powerful principle about God's presence and humankind's stewardship. God is God. He moves on His own terms. Yes, He involves us. Yes, we are co-laborers with Him and joint-heirs with Christ. Yes, we are friends of God. This is all true. But at the day's end, we must weigh all these realities in light of the fact that God is God. He is God Almighty, who inhabits eternity (see Is. 57:15 KJV). I want whatever *He* wants. His definition of revival must be mine; otherwise I will be tempted to adjust what He is doing to suit my preferences. This is happening across the earth today. Since Pentecost, the Holy Spirit has been poured out. We have a choice to make: Will we embrace this outpouring on God's terms, or will we try to "steady the cart" and adapt what God is doing to accommodate our systems?

WHAT KILLS REVIVAL?

Revival dies for a number of reasons. One of the main ones is humankind's poor stewardship of the Holy Spirit's activity. In fact, this is the reason many people do not experience the true fire of revival to begin with. The Holy Spirit broods over a community, church, or region looking for the man or woman who will say what God is saying and embrace what He is doing. We see this perfectly illustrated in the Creation account in Genesis 1.

> **God looks to see how His people will respond to the move of His presence.**

In Genesis 1:2, we note that "the Spirit of God was hovering over the face of the waters." He was present, but He only moved in creative power when the word of the Lord was spoken. This is how the Trinity operates—in complete and absolute unity. The Spirit does whatever the Father declares. They are absolutely in sync with one another. In revival, the Spirit moves wherever there are people who are thinking, saying, and moving in alignment with the Father. This is not some call to perfectionism. The Spirit doesn't require our perfect performance to work with; He simply needs willingness to yield to whatever the Father wants to do. This is not to say character is unimportant. Quite the contrary: Christ-like character is imperative to sustaining a Christ-like anointing in revival. The fact is, God uses ordinary, broken, humble people to accomplish His purposes. In being such yielded vessels, we will not dare try to touch what God is doing. Even if we don't fully understand everything that comes with revival, we will celebrate the Spirit's presence in our midst rather than shutting down what we consider uncomfortable.

Again, Second Samuel 6 illustrates how serious it is for us to keep our hands off a move of God's Spirit. Yes, we pastor it. Of course, church leaders need to assume a stewardship over a season of outpouring. At the same time, we cannot cry out for revival on our terms and conditions. Do you know what we will get? Nothing.

Or worse, the Spirit of God may noticeably move in our community, and immediately we make decisions that shut down His activity. God looks to see how His people will respond to the move of His presence. Will we embrace revival and everything that comes with it, or will we be like Uzzah and try to *steady the cart*. This language so vividly captures how many feel when the Holy Spirit begins to move. It is uncomfortable. People respond unusually. There are often dramatic manifestations as the Holy Spirit touches people and convicts their hearts. Because these things are so foreign to us, we get nervous and immediately look for some "big red button" to press that will shut everything down. We want revival without the mess. This is impossible.

This is not to say that we embrace disorder and chaos. Certainly not. However, we must consider revival so precious, so priceless that we are willing to take the bad with the good, and learn how to navigate through the strange.

ARE WE OUT OF ORDER?

Continuing on this subject of order and disorder in revival, we would do well to carefully review what the Apostle Paul considered to be *order*.

Many cite First Corinthians 14:40, where Paul reminds the church in Corinth that "all things should be done decently and in order." Absolutely. Here is my question: What does order look like from Paul's context? Verse 40 is the concluding passage in an entire chapter about the operation of spiritual gifts in a corporate gathering—namely the two more controversial manifestations of tongues and prophecy.

> **We do not evaluate the genuineness of revival by manifestations; we evaluate by life transformation.**

Paul's paradigm of "decently and in order" was not the complete absence of supernatural activity in corporate gatherings or in our Christian lives. Far from it. He was not urging the Corinthians to shut down the move of the Spirit, but rather to pastor and steward it. He was not even telling them to "take it outside," as many do today. Many of us believe in the move of the Spirit theologically, but when it comes to the *expression* of His presence and power, we encourage people to keep *that Holy Spirit stuff* in their small groups, or we schedule "renewal services" at times when no one could possibly attend the meetings, certain that we do not frighten Sunday-morning people away. I don't want our false idea of decently and in order to deceive us right out of an encounter with the glory of God. It's Scriptural language we use to justify our desire to be in control—to regulate the untamable Spirit of God. Truth be told, the Bible never tells us that the Holy Spirit is a gentleman. But one thing is for sure: He is the ultimate personification of good. Let's put it this way: If Jesus considered the Holy Spirit to be the best gift imaginable (see Luke 11:13), then we are safe to trust in His ways, even if they are unusual.

The question we must always ask is *what is the fruit?* If Jesus is being exalted and souls are being genuinely saved, we must recognize the presence of the Holy Spirit in the midst of what we might find chaotic, confusing, and outside of our comfort zones. If lives are radically transformed by a supernatural touch of God's power, it does not matter what kind of "package" the encounter comes in. If someone ends up laughing hysterically, lying prostrate on the floor for hours, shaking, crying, or shouting, we have no right to judge. These are simply evidences of the human flesh responding to the supernatural touch of God's presence. We do not evaluate the genuineness of revival by manifestations; we evaluate by life transformation. If people's encounters with God—however odd or unusual—serve as launching pads for living transformed lifestyles, we should celebrate, not scrutinize.

WHEN HOLY CHAOS BREAKS OUT

What may appear like chaos to us in the twenty-first century Church might be complete order to God. When we read testimonies of the great revivals of old, we often witness a holy pandemonium breaking out. Consider how George Whitefield describes one instance of his preaching the Gospel in Edinburgh, Scotland, in 1742:

> Such a commotion was surely never heard of, especially about eleven o'clock at night. It far outdid anything I ever saw in America. For about an hour and a half there was such weeping, so many felling into deep distress, and manifest it in various ways, that description is impossible. The people seemed to be smitten in scores. They were carried off and brought into the house like wounded soldiers taken from a field of battle. Their agonies and cries were deeply effecting.[1]

Christians from various traditions and multiple denominations celebrate the evangelistic efforts of Whitefield, recognizing him as a vital firebrand for spiritual awakening. Yet when we review specific instances where he preached the Gospel and witnessed mass conversions, we continually read of "disorderly" scenes such as the one above.

Let us move on to John Wesley, the founder of Methodism and a great pioneer for itinerant evangelism. He often preached to over five thousand people during his 7:00 A.M. Sunday morning service. Revival historian Wesley Duewel describes the scene of Wesley's church service in the following terms:

> Well-dressed, mature people suddenly cried out as if in the agonies of death. Both men and women, outside and inside the church buildings, would tremble and sink to the ground.[2]

It is impossible for us to cry out for revival, as in the days of old, and then be disappointed when the days-of-old manifestations start happening. Again, God has a higher concept of "decently and in order" than we do. Don't be surprised if what seems foolish at first glance is the very power of God moving in your midst, bringing healing, deliverance, and salvation.

WHEN WE DIE NEXT TO REVIVAL

This brings us back to Second Samuel 6, where Uzzah tries to steady the Ark. When we try to steady the move of God, we run the risk of missing revival, thus dying to the glorious things God has planned for our lives, churches, cities, and so on. As a result of Uzzah's sin, he died. Scripture does not reveal anything about Uzzah's intentions for steadying the Ark; nor should we draw meaning when such is not clearly revealed. All we know is what he did and the dramatic consequence.

Here is what we do see: God makes a very clear point about His presence and humanity's tendency to want to control it. If we truly desire the life and visitation of revival, we will align ourselves with what God is doing rather than manipulate His work to fit our vision of Christianity. Revival is the unceasing mercy of God, sovereignly reaching out to humankind and calling us to embrace *His* definition of what the Christian life looks like. This is why revival is often so confrontational. It confronts apathy and complacency, for sure.

God will not send revival to those who have an agenda to control His activity and movement. In fact, many communities *die* beside the ark of God. What does this mean? The Holy Spirit wants to move powerfully, but due to tradition, religion, desire to please people, the fear of man—a number of factors—we reject God's invitation for revival. As a result, we say a costly no to the move of His Spirit, continue on with spiritual "business as usual," and, sadly, die *right beside* the possibility of tremendous outpouring. The Spirit is willing; it is we who tell him no, or "I want it on my terms," or "I want it *this way*."

When all is said and done, we must be ready to answer this pivotal question: Whom do I want to make comfortable with my life or in my church—God or man? How we answer this determines whether we are qualified for the outpouring of revival. This determines everything.

NOTES

1. Albert D. Belden, *George Whitefield—The Awakener* (London: Sampson Low), 65.

2. Wesley Duewel, *Revival Fires* (Grand Rapids: Zondervan, 1995), 77.

CHAPTER 19

OVERCOME THE THREE HINDRANCES TO REVIVAL

PASTOR JOHN KILPATRICK

When the question is asked: "What hinders revival?"
one of the simple answers is this: We do not have
men and women who are prepared to pay the same
price to preach the same message and have the same
power as those revivalists of the past. Without these
firm believers, the community can never be changed.
Our concern is conciliatory, our obedience optional,
our lack theologically and culturally justified.
Quite simply, it costs too much!
—WINKIE PRATNEY

The three greatest hindrances to revival start with *pride*. Pride keeps you from humbling yourself and becoming absolutely desperate for revival. Pride assumes you have everything you need. Pride says, "I don't need to go *there* to get something from God." Pride's goal is to wage war against your desperation, as it makes you more aware of how *you* might look than what you could experience from one touch in God's glory. You might consider pride a "glory robber."

When you have pride, you see differently. The sights and sounds of revival become offensive to you. You look at people who are being touched dramatically by God, and you think to yourself, "I'd never do that. I'll never look like that." Pride is the very roadblock that prevents people from experiencing the touch they so desperately need. This is because pride assumes that man's definition and understanding of God is, in some ways, superior. It's not. Although we have access to great theological knowledge, we must live like children before the Lord. To assume we know *everything* about how He moves is the height of arrogance.

The second hindrance is the *fear of man*. When you are desperate enough for God, you don't care what people think about you. You understand that going deeper in God is costly, and it is worth whatever price you need to pay. One way to evaluate our progress in the Lord is to assess the desperation level of our closest friends. If they are simply "coasting" for God, not desiring to fulfill His purposes for their lives, it would seem that *you* have not become desperate enough. If your cry for personal revival is all-consuming, I guarantee that the people who invest most intimately and personally into your life *will* reflect this cry. If not, change is going to need to take place. If you genuinely burn with desperation for revival, those who are not as passionate for God will fall out of your life by default. They want to live comfortably, and your fire brings discomfort to them. When you go after God, you may lose close friends because they are satisfied living at a level that has become dissatisfying to you. It doesn't matter what people think. You don't pursue God based on what other people are doing or not doing. You press past the fear of man because you are desperate for a new taste of God's glory in your life.

In church settings, some people will *not* go to revival if their pastor says something like, "I wouldn't go to that revival, if I were you." But if you are desperate enough for God's touch and you become hungry enough for His presence, you will lose friends, lay down your reputation, and do whatever it takes to be touched by the Holy Spirit. Desperation says, "I don't care what my friends say. I don't care if I lose all my friends. I've got to go after God, no matter what."

You don't care what anybody thinks about you. Often the key to overcoming the fear of man is to make the unpopular decisions when God calls you to step out. Too many of us are content living in the shallows when the Spirit is beckoning us into deeper waters. We stay in the shallows because of fear. Our friends are there. Our comfort zones are there. Our reputation and acceptance are there. But what is more important? How hungry are you for God's touch in your life?

The third thing—the one that is, quite possibly, the *greatest* hindrance to revival—is *tolerated sin in our lives*. This is responsible for the addictions, strongholds, and bondages we live under. We don't like it. We are tired of living below instead of above. We know that being enslaved to sin is not God's best plan for our lives. The problem? The sin has become so familiar to us that we are not quite ready to part with it. It's almost as if we are afraid to live outside the confines of our prison cells because we have never lived *that way* before. *That way* is freedom. Sustained sin prevents sustained revival.

This is what desperation looks like: "I'm so desperate to get relief from this sin, I'm so desperate to be free from this lust, I'm so desperate to be free from drugs or alcohol, I'm so desperate to be free from gossip, pride, and bondage that *I can't live like this anymore.* I see who I am, and I've got to be touched by God because His touch will change everything!" It's this kind of desperation that will position you to break out of your bondage and experience the power of God you hunger for.

> **Too many of us are content living in the shallows when the Spirit is beckoning us into deeper waters.**

If you are really truly desperate, God will not disappoint you. If you're hungry, He's going to lead you to His banqueting table. He's not going to make you hungry the rest of your life. He is the One who deposited the hunger in you to begin with! Jesus said, "Blessed are you who hunger now, for you will be satisfied" (Luke 6:21 NIV) God is not a sadist. He's not going to make you hungry and then not feed you.

At the day's end, I can't *make* you hungry. I can inspire you and I can tell you stories, but if I say or write something and *God* starts to make you hungry, you won't be able to shake it until you are filled. That's the key. It's a spiritual thing. It's not a mind thing. It's not a carnal thing. It's not hype or excitement. It's a deep, interior work of the Holy Spirit moving on your heart. He is the only One capable of igniting and sustaining a burning hunger within you.

CHAPTER 20

DRAW LIFE FROM THE WELL OF YOUR ENCOUNTERS

PASTOR JOHN KILPATRICK

Revival cannot be organized, but we can set our sails to catch the wind from heaven when God chooses to blow upon His people once again.
—G. CAMPBELL MORGAN

Y ou can never put people above the presence of God. This may sound like a strange statement, especially to pastors and ministers. We know that "God so loved the world that he gave his only Son, that whoever believes in him shall not perish but have eternal life" (John 3:16). There is no question that God passionately loves people. It's when we put the demands of people above the desire to pursue God's presence that disqualifies us to offer these very people *anything* of true, eternal substance. People are not looking for the world repackaged. They are stepping into a church, hoping in some deep way that they will experience a *sanctuary* from the world they are inundated with day after day. We offer something the world does *not*—the Holy Spirit. A. W. Tozer once said, "Let me never become a slave to the crowds." As we cater to God's presence, we become most effective at serving God's people, for only the Holy Spirit can produce change, break bondages, deliver the oppressed, heal the sick, and conform us into the image of Christ.

We cannot elevate this idea of people having an enjoyable church experience to a place above the possibility of them having life-transforming encounters in God's presence. His presence is the only thing of any substance we offer the world. Our sermons don't cut it; the world can hear motivational talks from any number of life coaches and gurus. Our music is not the hallmark; without encountering God's presence, we're simply offering Christian entertainment and rock concerts. Our sanctuaries and structures may impress for a moment, but the world trumps the church in offering much more impressive buildings, venues, and concert halls.

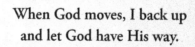

**When God moves, I back up
and let God have His way.**

God's presence *must* be our greatest priority. When He is our pursuit, we not only position ourselves to experience revival, but we begin to have access to the wellspring of life that will satisfy us through the dry seasons.

DON'T TRY TO MANUFACTURE REVIVAL

This is not to say that we can manufacture revival whenever and wherever we feel like it. If you have ever experienced the power of revival and you loved it so dearly because of how awesome it was, you will be tempted to step in, put your hand on it, and make it happen through your own efforts. This approach is worse than never having revival to begin with because now you're trying to make it up. You're trying to work up the speaking in tongues or manifestation of spiritual gifts. You're trying to preach with great unction. You're trying to whip up things in your life or in the church, and it just turns people off. It comes off as fake because it is, even though it is motivated by a desire for revival. This where we quickly get into the flesh. Our version of revival will always be a very sad, substandard imitation of the glorious real thing.

When God moves, I back up and let God have His way. If He's not moving in an extraordinary way, I step up and preach. I do the very best I can, but I never put my hand to it and try to manufacture something that's not there.

DRAW FROM THE WELL OF YOUR PERSONAL ENCOUNTERS

This brings up the question: *Is it possible to sustain revival in my life?* You cannot manufacture the experience of revival, but you can remember your encounters *in* revival. It is remembering the testimony of what God has done that reminds you of who God is and what He can do again, and it releases faith to believe for a greater outpouring in the future.

While the winds of revival are blowing, you can have such powerful and profound encounters with God that you'll have those moments to draw from throughout the rest of your life. They are epic encounters that will keep catapulting you forward, even when the wind is not blowing. You are *not* manufacturing anything. You are using the gift of memory to draw spiritual nutrients from your history of encounters with God.

Your encounters with God possess an innate capacity to hold and sustain you spiritually. The key is remembering what God has done. Time after time, Scripture calls us to *remember* the works of the Lord. This produces thanksgiving. It releases praise. We are rejuvenated by a vision of the God who moves and touches His people with great power.

> **You cannot manufacture the experience of revival, but you can remember your encounters *in* revival.**

If you have ever been burned by touching a stove, I promise you, you're not going back to touch that stove again. You have enough memory of that burn to alter the course of your life moving forward. You're not going to touch that stove again because of that memory. Memory is a powerful thing. When you have an encounter with God and you remember it, that memory is accompanied by different feelings, emotions, sounds, pictures, images, and sensations. By remembering your encounters with God, it's like you are immediately transported back to that destiny-defining moment to experience it all over again.

PETER'S MEMORY OF ENCOUNTER

When Peter denied the Lord Jesus, the Bible says he denied Him by coal and fire (see John 18:15-18 KJV). Peter denied Jesus three times by a "fire of coals" or a "charcoal fire." Scripture didn't say this denial took place by a fire of wood; John specifically indicated that it was by a "fire of coals."

When Jesus rose from the dead, He found Peter fishing alongside Nathanael, the sons of Zebedee, and two other disciples (see John 21:1-3). We watch the following scene unfold:

Just as day was breaking, Jesus stood on the shore; yet the disciples did not know that it was Jesus. Jesus said to them, "Children, do you have any fish?" They answered him, "No." He said to them, "Cast the net on the right side of the boat, and you will find some." So they cast it, and now they were not able to haul it in, because of the quantity of fish. That disciple whom Jesus loved therefore said to Peter, "It is the Lord!"

When Simon Peter heard that it was the Lord, he put on his outer garment, for he was stripped for work, and threw himself into the sea. The other disciples came in the boat, dragging the net full of fish, for they were not far from the land, but about a hundred yards off.

When they got out on land, they saw a charcoal fire in place, with fish laid out on it, and bread (John 21:4-9).

Pay attention to that final verse. When they got back to land, they saw a *charcoal fire*. A fire of coals, just like the one that was close to Peter when he denied the Lord Jesus.

They cooked the fish on that fire of coals. Coal has a distinctive, pungent smell. A memory of July Fourth or Memorial Day cookouts can instantly resurface when you smell that charcoal, regardless of what season you're currently in. It could the dead of winter. All it takes is one smell of those *coals of fire* to bring you back to the hamburgers and hotdogs you cooked on the grill during summertime.

When Peter came to the shore, Jesus had built the fire of coals. The smell likely took him right back to that courtyard encounter when he denied the Lord. Jesus didn't have to say a word. The smell had the potential to bring Peter into a grace-filled, restorative encounter with Jesus *through a memory*. The story concludes with Peter's restoration and, really, his preparation. He is restored to ministry and prepared for the incredible days that are ahead. The catalyst that brought Peter to this destiny-defining moment *was likely* his memory of what happened when he denied Jesus. There is a good chance that those coals of fire brought him right back to that place. The power of our senses is amazingly strong.

When you have an encounter with God, it has a fragrance that goes with it. It has a feeling that accompanies it. There are emotions that come alongside it. These sensations aren't meant to just be experienced *during* the encounter; they linger long after that moment has passed. They are like the smell of charcoal that instantly brings us back to a Memorial Day cookout. Maybe it's a song. Perhaps it's a specific place. You might have received a prophetic word. The Holy Spirit has a supernatural way of making one encounter become another encounter all over again through the power of memory. Your history of encounters with God is full of memories that the Holy Spirit will refresh over and over in your life. He does this to keep you hungry for more of His presence and to press into everything God has made available to you in His Kingdom.

CHAPTER 21

PURSUE INTIMACY WITH JESUS

DR. MICHAEL BROWN

*It is one of the ironies of the ministry that
the very man who works in God's name is
often hardest put to find time for God. The
parents of Jesus lost Him at church, and they
were not the last ones to lose Him there.*
—VANCE HAVNER

For many years, I have told students at our ministry school that
the greatest challenge they will face is not learning to teach or
preach well, or to administrate or evangelize, or walk in the Spirit's
power, or raise funds, or whatever else is needed for effective ministry. Instead, the greatest challenge for those of us in ministry, not to

mention for all believers, is to maintain a solid, consistent, personal devotional life. Failing that, we fail where it counts most. And yet the more successful the ministry, the harder it can be to break away from the demands and the busyness and simply focus our attention on meeting with the Lord.

Recently, after completing another whirlwind ministry schedule (teaching from 9:00 A.M. to 6:00 P.M. for three straight days, doing two hours of live radio in the middle of two of those days, plus writing at night), I met with two of our grads, who had with them a book called *Personal Revival* written by my friend S. J. Hill.

They reminded me that I had written the foreword to the book, and so I opened it, saying to them half-jokingly that I wanted to see if I was convicted by my own words. I was!

Back in 1999, I wrote these words, which seem timelier than ever:

> If there is one thing I have learned in the last twenty-eight years it is that everything flows out of our personal relationship with the Lord, that the inner life is more essential than the outward life, that our private walk with God is more important than our public ministry for God, that personal revival takes precedence over corporate revival. After all, the Body of Christ is made up of individuals, and it will never be stronger as a unit than it is individually.
>
> Yet it is so tempting to put all our emphasis on the works of ministry—preaching, teaching, pastoring, leading worship, leading a home group, witnessing, visiting the sick, being godly parents, going on mission trips, making disciples—and it is so easy to neglect our private devotion to the Lord. (A more subtle temptation is to spend all our private time in prayer and the Word preparing for our

public, outward ministry responsibilities.) What about intimacy with Jesus for the sake of intimacy? What about deepening our relationship with the Master simply for the sake of that relationship? What about pursuing the imitation of God in our lives as a goal in itself and not just as a tool for more effective ministry?

The problem, of course, is that the responsibilities of life and ministry often carry us along with the force of their demands, driving us to action and away from devotion, pushing us to work for the Lord but pulling us away from waiting on the Lord. How can we resist this tendency? How can we make our relationship with God the highest priority of our lives? How can we experience personal revival, and how can we sustain that life of passion, fire, and renewal?

Of course, our works for the Lord are important. We are called to win souls, to set captives free, to bear fruit that will last, to make an impact for the King. But if our foundations are not secure and our roots are not deep, many of our works will go up in flames.

You see, it is possible to backslide while preaching to thousands. It is possible to grow cold while serving in a red-hot revival. It is possible to leave your first love while working for Jesus on the mission field...and so we must learn to maintain personal revival in the valley as well as on the mountaintop.

One of the most striking passages in the Gospels is found in Luke 5, where, as a result of Jesus's miracles, "great crowds gathered to hear him and to be healed of their infirmities. But he would withdraw to desolate places and pray" (Luke 5:15-16).

How extraordinary. These people wanted to hear what Jesus had to say, and they needed to be healed. And Jesus had what they needed. And He was often moved by compassion to heal the sick, which would have pulled Him to the crowds, not away from them. Yet "he would withdraw to desolate places and pray."

What does this say to us, especially those of us who seem to have an endless stream of people to minister to and needs to meet? (All this has only been multiplied in the digital age and through social media. The Lord once said to me, "Why do you have time to answer all your emails, but you don't have time for Me?" Today, who can even answer all their emails?)

If Jesus could break away from the needs of the crowds and pray, why can't we? If meeting with His Father was more important to Jesus than meeting with the crowds (or being with family or friends or working a job), why isn't it more important to us? And if He needed that time alone with God, don't we need it a thousand times more?

Note well what Luke records next: "On one of those days, as he was teaching, Pharisees and teachers of the law were sitting there, who had come from every village of Galilee and Judea and from Jerusalem. And the power of the Lord was with him to heal" (Luke 5:17).

The Lord's empowered ministry flowed directly out of His time with His Father, and, more importantly, He did not lose intimacy with His Father for the sake of a successful ministry. And while it is true that we are called to sacrifice many things in our service for the Lord, one of those things is not our intimate, personal relationship with Him.

So let's search our hearts and ask ourselves a simple question: What is the most important thing of all, and are we putting *that* first?

CHAPTER 22

ATMOSPHERE + CLIMATE = CULTURE

PASTOR JOHN KILPATRICK

*A revival, then, really means days
of heaven upon earth.*
—D. MARTYN LLOYD-JONES

Revival is uniquely God-birthed and produces supernatural results in our lives. We cannot create revival, but we *can* steward it well when it comes. We all want to see revival continue. We want to live out these days of Heaven on earth where the demonstration of God's power becomes the norm, not the exception. We want to live lives that carry the Spirit's power and are fueled by passion for Jesus. We are not content with getting a touch from God then going home, only to live the same old way we did *before* getting touched. Those days are over.

There is a hunger in this hour to see the move of God *sustained* from generation to generation. What is the key? Atmosphere plus climate equals culture. This was one of the first things I learned during revival.

When the Holy Spirit first broke out at Brownsville, there were about ten days before the United States, and then the world, started coming to our church. At this point, I knew everyone in the church. I knew their stories and their struggles. During this ten-day window, I recall several occasions when we stayed at the church all night long. I said goodbye to Steve Hill after sunrise the next day on one of these occasions.

> **We cannot be content with receiving a touch from God in the confines of a building or meeting. Our desire must be to *respond* to the Spirit's touch by readjusting our lives.**

I remember seeing entire families lying on the floor, tears streaming down their faces. In that atmosphere of revival, the Holy Spirit was doing a powerful healing work in their hearts. He was restoring marriages where the husbands had been unfaithful. He was restoring prodigal children to their parents. It was not uncommon to see teenagers lying on the ground, loving on their parents. Truly, this was a supernatural atmosphere. There was such a relaxed spirit in the church as the fire of revival burned away the religion and formality. During those nights I watched the presence of God authentically and powerfully touch these people. They could *not* have faked such deep encounters.

Then I started to hear the reports. People experienced freedom, healing, and joy during revival, but by the time their cars entered the driveways back at their homes, they started fighting again. The same foul language permeated the atmosphere of their homes. The same filthy programs and pornographic images were displayed on their televisions. Wives continued to emasculate their husbands, and husbands continued to beat down their wives. If I heard it once, I heard it one hundred times—the same people who were laying on the church floor during revival were fighting like cats and dogs when they got back to their homes. I asked the Lord, "What is going on here?"

He reminded me of how we prayed for two and a half years to purge the atmosphere at the church—we prayed until the heavens opened and the glory came. When those people came into that atmosphere, it changed their personality. They became loving, compassionate, and conciliatory. But when they drove back home, they stepped into in the old atmospheres that had not been purged. They returned to comfort zones of sin, immorality, contention, pride, lust, and bondage. Those things are *not* comfortable in the weighty presence of God, which explains why they experienced temporary reprieve during revival. We cannot be content with receiving a touch from God in the confines of a building or meeting. Our desire must be to *respond* to the Spirit's touch by readjusting our lives. He melts our hearts through a divine work of grace. From that point onward, we cannot expect that, automatically, our lives will become saintly. We need to collaborate with the Spirit through obedience to God and yielding to the Word. Revival is designed to make these disciplines *easier* because we have been so deeply touched by God's presence. After being saturated in an atmosphere of this presence, where the heavens are opened and there is a continuous stream of His glory, we must get off the floor, get into our cars, and say yes to the same Holy Spirit who touched us so deeply during the revival service.

The Lord told me, "My people are more a product of their atmosphere than they care to admit." Atmosphere is very important to us, both individually and corporately. It affects the way we feel, how we perform, how we think, how we sleep, our intimacy—everything about us. If we want to sustain a lifestyle of revival—in our lives and in our churches—we need to identify how atmosphere impacts every area of our daily lives. It's not enough just to visit a place that has a certain atmosphere; our goal is to carry this atmosphere into every area our lives just like Jesus did. The truth is, we have received the same Holy Spirit that Jesus had, and this is what makes it possible for us to live out what Jesus exemplified. Look at Jesus's discussion with Nathanael,

> Nathanael answered him, "Rabbi, you are the Son of God! You are the King of Israel!" Jesus answered him, "Because I said to you, 'I saw you under the fig tree,' do you believe? You will see greater things than these." And he said to him, "Truly, truly, I say to you, you will see heaven opened, and the angels of God ascending and descending on the Son of Man." (John 1:49-51)

Jesus lived under an open Heaven. He told Nathanael that he should expect to see a continuous flow of supernatural power, resources, and ability streaming from Heaven to earth through Jesus. Angels would come to His aid and depart from Him to accomplish assignments. When Jesus came, the earth lived under a brass Heaven. There was a period of prophetic silence preceding the birth of Jesus. For even longer still—since Adam fell in the Garden—humankind did *not* have general access to God's presence. Throughout the Old Testament, God selected certain individuals to carry out His redemptive plans in the world. He chose some, not all. Jesus made *all* a possibility. Now, *whosoever* believes in Him can be born again, receive the Holy Spirit, live under an open Heaven, and carry Heaven's atmosphere wherever he or she goes.

Jesus came to show us how it was to be done. It is possible for each one of us to carry this same atmosphere because He made every provision necessary for us to live under an open Heaven, just as He did. We received the same Holy Spirit at Jesus. The goal now is to carry Heaven's atmosphere in our lives and in our churches so that we see the atmosphere produce a climate and, ultimately, create a culture. This is the progression.

ATMOSPHERE

An *atmosphere* can be defined as the air of a place. Your atmosphere is what defines your surroundings. Let me give you a few illustrations of familiar atmospheres. Think of Florida. The normal atmosphere is warm and sunny. Conversely, think of Aspen, Colorado. There, the normal atmosphere is cold and snowy. What atmosphere are you living under? We are either following the Spirit or following the flesh. There is no middle ground. Even though our pursuit after God will experience some "abnormalities" or mistakes along the journey, our hearts remain bent toward following Him, no matter what the cost. Even though Florida occasionally has abnormal cold fronts, the predominant atmosphere is warm and sunny. May the same be said of your walk in the Spirit. Follow the Spirit's voice. Pursue holiness. Obey the Word. We create this atmosphere, not just by being in an environment where the Holy Spirit is moving, but also by becoming an environment that He is free to move in and through.

CLIMATE

Climate is a sustained atmosphere. Florida's atmosphere produces a climate conducive to growing fruit such as oranges and grapefruits. Aspen's climate, on the other hand, is not welcoming to these types of fruit. The dominant atmosphere always defines the climate. Likewise, the atmosphere you live under determines what kind of fruit your life or ministry produces. If you are desperate to live every moment under the Holy Spirit's influence, your atmosphere will create a climate conducive to producing the fruit of the Spirit and the gifts of the Spirit. You will walk in His character and power. Your sustained atmosphere determines whether you see evidence of the Spirit's presence at work in your life. This is why people could be touched at Brownsville, but return home unchanged. They enjoyed the touch of God, but were unwilling to completely submit to the Holy Spirit's work and see what they experienced in church become sustained in everyday life.

> **The atmosphere you live under determines what kind of fruit your life or ministry produces.**

CULTURE

This is a way of life that is built around a specific climate. Because of Florida's climate, beachgoers, tourists, boaters, and fishermen define the culture. Likewise, Colorado has developed a culture of skiing because of its climate. Culture is the by-product of climate. The culture is ultimately what draws in the people. As our lives and churches sustain a climate of revival, we have the potential to create a supernatural culture that impacts the world around us. Many talk about creating a *revival culture*. We cannot build a culture unless we first establish the infrastructure; otherwise people will continue to be touched by God but remain unchanged. When we sustain a climate in which the gifts of the

Spirit become normative, the fruit of the Spirit defines our character, the power of God flows freely, the lost experience freedom in God's presence, and life is built *around* the Holy Spirit; we create a revolutionary, supernatural culture. This is the end goal of revival. We are no longer human centered, but Spirit centered. We no longer build churches to please man, but we orient everything toward pleasing God. In our personal lives, it's not about following the latest cultural trends, defining our perspective based on popular media, or mimicking the style of Hollywood; we build our lives around the Holy Spirit. He decides what is normal and what is abnormal, not people. Not popular culture. Not the world. Not Christian gimmicks.

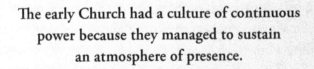

> The early Church had a culture of continuous
> power because they managed to sustain
> an atmosphere of presence.

Famed preacher Martyn Lloyd-Jones said, "We should be anxious to see something happening that will arrest the nations, all the peoples, and cause them to stop and to think again." This will not happen if we do not change the atmosphere of our lives, families, and churches. We celebrate what God does in our church buildings and during our meetings; however, we want to see that atmosphere sustained outside the four walls in order to create a climate that ultimately produces a revival culture.

The early Church experienced an atmosphere change on the Day of Pentecost. This was not an isolated touch. What was the key to the supernatural culture that the early Church walked in, where miracles, deliverances, and mass salvations occurred on a regular basis?

And they devoted themselves to the apostles' teaching and the fellowship, to the breaking of bread and the prayers. And awe came upon every soul, and many wonders and signs were being done through the apostles. And all who believed were together and had all things in common. And they were selling their possessions and belongings and distributing the proceeds to all, as any had need. And day by day, attending the temple together and breaking bread in their homes, they received their food with glad and generous hearts, praising God and having favor with all the people. And the Lord added to their number day by day those who were being saved (Acts 2:42-47).

Moving forward, the first church community *devoted themselves* to the apostles' teaching and fellowship. They made radical lifestyle adjustments to accommodate what God was doing, rather than just adding Him to their already busy lives. He was the center of everything. He was top priority. His Spirit was paramount. The Word was final and definitive. The early Church had a culture of continuous power because they managed to sustain an atmosphere of presence.

CHAPTER 23

A NEW JESUS REVOLUTION

DR. MICHAEL BROWN

After Christ was risen from the dead the apostles
went out to preach His message, and what they
preached was the cross. And wherever they went into
the wide world they carried the cross, and the same
revolutionary power went with them. The radical
message of the cross transformed Saul of Tarsus and
changed him from a persecutor of Christians to a
tender believer and an apostle of the faith. Its power
changed bad men into good ones. It shook off the long
bondage of paganism and altered completely the whole
moral and mental outlook of the Western world.
—A. W. Tozer

To the core of my being, I am a revolutionary. I eat, drink, breathe, and sleep revolution. *This* is what a revived life is called to become.

Revolution is in my blood, and it is in my blood because of Jesus, the ultimate revolutionary, the One who came into this world to bring about radical, dramatic, sweeping change through His death, resurrection, teaching, example, and empowerment. I cannot separate Jesus from revolution any more than I can separate Jesus from redemption and reconciliation.

When I think of revolution, I think of radical, dramatic, sweeping change. I think of overthrowing the status quo. I think of out with the old, in with the new. For the most part, when the world does it, it is violent. It's bloody. It's replacing one bad system with another bad system. But a Jesus revolution is transformation through the Gospel.

It is overcoming evil with good. It is overcoming hatred with love. It is overcoming lies with truth. Rather than taking life, it gives life. So for me, when revival really spreads and really has its affect, when the Church is radically changed, then the culture will be impacted. Jesus changes us, and we change our world.

In the midst of the Brownsville Revival, God started to burden me with the message of revolution and the vision of revolution—a new Jesus revolution. Revival and revolution go hand in hand. When the Church is truly revived, it will have a revolutionary impact on the culture. When sinners are radically saved, it will have a revolutionary impact on the culture. On the flip side, we cannot have this revolutionary impact unless we are revivalists. God's people must first be touched by His presence and power; otherwise we'll just be striving with our own effort.

Jesus did not come into this world to leave things as they were, and the final commission He gave to His disciples (known as the Great Commission) was a call to change the world with Him.

As noted by Christian teacher H. S. Vigeveno, "Our world has witnessed many a revolution, but none as effective as the one that divided history into B.C. and A.D.... Revolutionary, indeed, this mission, to begin with a cross and sway the whole world through suffering love."

Or in the words of the German theologian Gerhard Lohfink, "It is true that Jesus never called for a political, revolutionary transformation of Jewish society. Yet the repentance which he demanded as a consequence of his preaching of the reign of God sought to ignite within the people of God a movement in comparison to which the normal type of revolution is insignificant."

> **Jesus did not come into this world to leave things as they were.**

The revolution Jesus started—and the revolution I live for—is a revolution that overcomes hatred with love, violence with compassion, and lies with truth. Make no mistake about it: It is a radical revolution that brings about radical change, and as followers of Jesus, we are to be agents of radical change.

Where we see slavery and human trafficking, we are called to address it.

Where we see the slaughter of the unborn and assault on human dignity, we are called to address it.

Where we see sexual anarchy and the deterioration of morality, we are called to address it.

If we don't, who will? If we are not the salt of the earth and the light of the world (see Matt. 5:13-16), who will be?

If we don't take the lead in standing for justice in society, if we don't take the lead in modeling godly marriages and family life, if we don't take the lead in advocating for what is right and opposing what is wrong, who will?

Some would say, "You're mixing politics with religion."

In reply I say, "You're separating religion from daily life."

Some would say, "Jesus simply taught us to go and make disciples."

In reply I ask, "But how do disciples live?"

TWO REVOLUTIONS

My own life was dramatically impacted by two revolutions, one very negative and one very positive. The first was the counterculture revolution of the 1960s, when I plunged headlong into decadence and rebellion, playing drums in a rock band, using LSD at the age of fourteen, and shooting heroin at the age of fifteen.

Although I was bar mitzvahed in 1968 as a conservative Jew, for me, it was more of a cultural event than a spiritual event. The more impactful event that took place that year—I was just thirteen at the time—was seeing the Jimi Hendrix Experience in concert. Everything about the band—the sound and volume of the music, their flamboyant dress and hair styles, the message of the songs and the message of their lives—called out to me, and I followed along, quickly falling into the rebellion and anarchy that marked that era.

But in 1971 I was impacted by a very different revolution—the Jesus Revolution, featured in a famous *Time* magazine cover story in June of that same year. Suddenly around America and even around the globe, hippies, radicals, and rebels were getting dramatically converted, giving themselves to Jesus even more fervently than they had given themselves to sex, drugs, rock and roll, and Eastern religion. The impact on my life was nothing less than revolutionary.

Giving up drugs virtually overnight is revolutionary. Following Jesus as a Jew is revolutionary. Going from Led Zeppelin and the Grateful Dead to the Word of God—the Bible—is revolutionary.

IT IS POSSIBLE TO CHANGE HISTORY

What we need to do is look at God's standards in Scripture, at God's promises, and then read about other world changers. This will ignite our faith to believe that, no matter where God has placed us, *we* can also become revolutionaries in our unique spheres of influence.

I encourage you to read about others who have had a revolutionary effect on culture. Four days before John Wesley died, he wrote a letter to William Wilberforce, a member of Parliament. Wilberforce had come to faith through Wesley's ministry. Wilberforce had a twofold burden: 1) eradicating slavery and the slave trade from the British Empire, and 2) the reformation of morals.

> No matter where God has placed us, *we* can also become revolutionaries in our unique spheres of influence.

Wesley wrote that "unless God has raised you up for this very thing, you will be worn out by the opposition of men and devils. But if God be for you, who can be against you? Are all of them together stronger than God? O be not weary of well doing!" To paraphrase, Wesley basically told Wilberforce, "If God is with you, then not only can you see success here in England, but you can revolutionize America as well." And of course the rest is history.

History contains many testimonies of how things have changed in impossible ways. Something that looked utterly hopeless one day radically turned around. In the early 1960s, pollsters predicated a peaceful generation in America, submitted to authority. Their ambition was simply the fulfillment of the American Dream. Little did they know that it would be the most contentious generation in our nation's history—the generation of the counterculture revolution of sex, drugs, rock and roll, Eastern Religion, rebellion, and the generation gap. They didn't see that coming. They also didn't see the Jesus revolution coming in the midst of the counterculture revolution, where God began to save the most radical hippies, rebels, and offscouring of society. God began to bring us to Himself. That's when I came to faith—in 1971. I was a heroin-shooting, LSD-using, rebellious hippie rock drummer.

GOD ARISE!

In the midst of these impossible situations, God can arise, and God has arisen. So we need to stir our faith. We need to raise our standard. We need to say, "Okay, if I have to go against the culture, I'm going to do it. I am going to honor authority. I am going to be respectful toward those I differ from, but I am not going to bow down to the culture. I am not going to capitulate to the culture. I am only going to bow down to the Lord."

We have to recognize as followers of Jesus that we are called to swim against the tide. We are called to go against the grain, whatever the cost or consequence. Jesus says those who are going to be His disciples must deny themselves and take up the cross and then follow Him.

But the revolution cannot stop there. It must go beyond each of us individually to touch the world around us—the poor, the hurting, the lost, the confused, the rebellious, and the defiant.

We must stand boldly for the truth of the Gospel, not as advocates of a theocracy, as if we were seeking to forcibly impose biblical morality and faith on everyone else—that is not what we are about, and that is not what we advocate.

We must stand boldly and without shame as witnesses to the fact that God's ways are best, that they are ways of life and hope and restoration and freedom.

A leading socialist in the 1920s once said, "We socialists would have nothing to do if you Christians had continued the revolution begun by Jesus."

To each of you I say, let's get on with the Jesus revolution. If ever it was needed, it is today. But this revolution must be fueled by the fires of revival!

We have to recognize as followers of Jesus that we are called to swim against the tide.

HOW TO KEEP THE FIRE BURNING

How can we see revival sustained from generation to generation? We cannot let revival end with us. What we experience in the place of revival needs to so profoundly transform how we live that we cannot keep it contained.

D. L. Moody once asked, "What makes the Dead Sea dead? Because it is all the time receiving, never giving out anything. Why is it that many Christians are cold? Because they are all the time receiving, never giving out anything." Yes, revival brings supernatural refreshing to believers. It revitalizes our faith. It reignites our passion for God. But the key to sustaining this passion is dedicating our lives to become the revolutionary agents of change that our world desperately needs. How does this keep the fire burning? Simple. As we step into our revolutionary role, we are forced to place a continual demand on our faith. Following Jesus is not a theological concept; nor is it limited to the confines of a church sanctuary. We are walking it out, day after day. We are no longer living for ourselves. We don't see revival as something that adds sugary toppings to our me-centric flavor of the faith. In revival, we catch a fresh glimpse of who God is and the kind of powerful, transformational impact He desires to have in the world. How will He do this? Through you and me. We are the hands and feet of Jesus on the earth.

It is when the revivalists of one generation become the revolutionaries of the next that truly the fire will never sleep.

AFTERWORD

God never intended for revival to be an event or *just* an experience. We are mistaken when we start describing a revival's effectiveness simply based on how long church services and meetings continued on in a certain fixed location. Revival is not about buildings, meetings, or church services. A move of God's Spirit is not measured by the quantity of gatherings; its success rate is evaluated by the *quality* of Christianity produced in the lives of those who were impacted.

Several of the leaders at the International House of Prayer were impacted by what they experienced during the Brownsville Revival. This move of God continues even to this day—it continues in the missionaries who are taking the Gospel to the four corners of the earth whose lives were marked during the fires of revival. It continues through the intercessory missionaries in Kansas City and many others throughout our nation who labor for a sustained move of the Spirit in their cities and in the nations of the earth. It continues in homes, where husbands and wives are reconciled, sons and daughters are set free from addiction, and prodigals are brought home. It continues in those who live to see justice released throughout the earth, biblical values restored, and human trafficking brought to an end. What began on Father's Day back in 1995 can truly be described as a *Fire That Never Sleeps*.

This was truly a helpful and due-season book, as you received two important perspectives on the topic of revival. Dr. Michael Brown is a scholar of revival and John Kilpatrick is a pastor of revival. Dr. Brown painted a compelling vision for what revival looks like and why we need it, while Pastor Kilpatrick took us right into the reality of what he personally experienced during the Pensacola Outpouring. What you just read was not a memorial to what happened back in the 1990s; it was testimony of what God has done and is continuing to do in the lives of people who were touched back then.

Michael Brown opened the book by giving us a sobering yet hope-filled glimpse of where we are right now in modern-day society. He presented an urgent wake-up call to a Church that, all too often, lives beneath what Jesus paid so high a price for. Revival is about the restoration of true New Testament Christianity; it is about the Holy Spirit establishing the first commandment in first place in the lives of God's people.

John Kilpatrick then brought us right into the midst of the Brownsville Revival. He shared his testimony of how God prepared him for the revival, how the Holy Spirit gripped his heart for prayer, and, ultimately, how God desires to sustain an atmosphere of prayer and outpouring in our churches and lives today.

My hope is that this book ignited a desire in your heart to encounter God afresh, along with giving you practical ways that you can keep the fires of revival burning in your life today. The end goal is not just to produce impassioned worship or exciting church meetings. *The Fire That Never Sleeps* does not conclude with just firing up the Church; it ends with changing the world and people loving Jesus with all their heart and strength.

After all, that is the high vision of revival—*on earth as it is in Heaven.*

MIKE BICKLE
International House of Prayer Missions Base, Kansas City
Author of *Passion for Jesus* and *Growing in Prayer*

ABOUT THE AUTHORS

MICHAEL L. BROWN holds a PhD from New York University in Near Eastern languages and literature and is recognized as one of the leading Messianic Jewish scholars in the world today. He is the founder and president of FIRE School of Ministry, the host of the nationally syndicated daily talk radio show *The Line of Fire*, and the author of more than twenty-five books.

JOHN KILPATRICK was blessed to experience firsthand the Glory of God as Holy Spirit entrusted him with the pastoral oversight of the historic Brownsville Revival in Pensacola, Florida and the Bay Revival in Mobile, Alabama. An in-demand apostolic leader, speaker and author, Kilpatrick currently serves as the founder and senior pastor of Church of His Presence in Daphne, Alabama.

LARRY SPARKS is a conference speaker and author of the book *Breakthrough Faith*. He is a regular columnist for Charisma online and host of the radio program *Voice of Destiny*, and has been featured on the Christian Broadcasting Network and *It's Supernatural* with Sid Roth. He holds a Master of Divinity from Regent University

VISIT JOHN KILPATRICK MINISTRIES

johnkilpatrick.org

FOR ACCESS TO...

Media Library: Hours of free video teaching that will position you to experience more of God's revival fire in your life.

Prophetic Words and Blessings: Printable prophetic words and blessings given to John Kilpatrick from the Holy Spirit.

Event Schedule: See when John Kilpatrick will be ministering in a city near you.

ABOUT JOHN KILPATRICK

John Kilpatrick was blessed to experience firsthand the Glory of God as Holy Spirit entrusted him with the pastoral oversight of the historic Brownsville Revival in Pensacola, Florida and the Bay Revival in Mobile, Alabama. He currently serves as the founder and senior pastor of Church of His Presence in Daphne, Alabama. He also travels extensively across the nation spreading the fires of revival and impacts churches around the world through media ministry. With nearly fifty years of pastoral ministry, twenty-two of which included his ministry at Brownsville Assembly of God in Pensacola, Florida, he and his wife Brenda are fulfilling their apostolic call by helping to establish churches and mentoring ministers. His hunger and passion for God's presence awakens and stirs the hearts of many to cry out for a move of God.

ENCOUNTER.
ACTIVATE.
TRANSFORM.

EQUIP CULTURE MINISTRIES with LARRY SPARKS
WWW.LAWRENCESPARKS.COM

LARRY SPARKS is a speaker, curriculum director for Destiny Image Publishers, revivalist, and columnist for *Charisma Magazine*. **Featured on CBN, TBN, and Sid Roth's *It's Supernatural*,** Larry is passionate about raising up communities who usher in regional revival and awakening. He is committed to training the body of Christ through one of his **3 TRANSFORMATIVE SEMINARS:**

1. IGNITING A REVIVAL LIFESTYLE: Ideal for churches and conferences. Larry shares vital keys and transformative principles from revivalists and great awakening movements from throughout history—some popular and some that are hardly known about. From the birth of the New Testament Church until today, the Holy Spirit has been summoning the people of God back to a lifestyle marked by the presence and power of Jesus! The lessons you learn will help you experience God's supernatural power—personally and corporately—and sustain it, so revival can move beyond the church and become reformation!

2. REVIVAL IN MEDIA: Perfect for college campuses, schools of ministry, and arts schools. This seminar will equip Christians who believe they have been called into arts and media—film, music, art, theatre, dance, TV, writing. They will learn how to practically carry the creative presence of the Holy Spirit into that sphere of influence and become ambassadors for the Kingdom of God who change atmospheres through their work. It's not about Christians making more "Christian media." Instead, it's about Spirit-filled, Kingdom ambassadors representing the nature and character of God by releasing revival in media!

3. BREAKTHROUGH FAITH: This series will equip everyday Christians to practically put the Word of God to work in their lives and position themselves to experience sustained breakthrough. Jesus defined the normal Christian life as one where His followers not only received miracles; they actually released miracles that transformed the circumstances and environments around them! The secret to walking out this lifestyle is not some formula, blueprint or gimmick: it's about stepping into new levels of intimacy with God and enjoying greater access to the Holy Spirit's manifest Presence. From that foundation, you will build a lifestyle of victory by putting time-tested, Biblical truths to work and start walking in breakthrough faith!

You can visit Larry's website at **lawrencesparks.com**. Also, you can "like" Larry on **Facebook** (*LarryVSparks*) and **Twitter** (*@LarryVSparks*) to **receive empowerment keys to experience and sustain a revival lifestyle.**

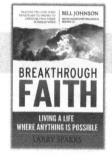